Graham Harvey won the BP Natural World Book Prize for *The Killing of the Countryside*. An agricultural graduate and journalist, he has written several critically acclaimed books, exposing the sometimes shady world of industrial food production. His passions for good food and a healthy, sustainable and vibrant countryside have kept him at the forefront of contemporary agricultural thinking for the past decade.

Graham Harvey is currently the Agricultural Story Editor for the BBC's long running radio drama, *The Archers*.

Praise for *Killing of the Countryside*:

"I fully support this book's profound and Blake-like charge".

JOHN FOWLES, SUNDAY TIMES

"A forceful, informed and authoritative account".

BRYN GREEN, SPECTATOR

"Absolute dynamite... It's so envigorating to hear the case for a truly sustainable, countryside-friendly agriculture".

JONATHON PORRITT, BBC WILDLIFE

Also by Graham Harvey
The Killing of the Countryside
The Forgiveness of Nature
Living Landscapes: Parkland
We Want Real Food

The Carbon Fields

How our countryside can save Britain

Graham Harvey

GrassRoots

PO Box 416, Pawlett, Bridgwater
Somerset. TA6 9EP

www.grassrootsfood.co.uk

First Published in the UK by Grass Roots,
an imprint of GrassRoots Food Ltd, 2008

A copy of the British Library Cataloguing in Publication Data
is available from the British Library

ISBN: 978-0-9560707-0-8

Printed and bound in the UK.

Every effort has been made to obtain the necessary permissions with
reference to copyrighted material, both illustrative and quoted
and contact details. We apologise for any omissions in this respect
and will be pleased to make the appropriate acknowledgments
and changes in any future edition

Grass Roots is committed to a sustainable future in all aspects
of our business, our readers & our environment.
The book you are holding is made from paper from
sustainably managed forests.

To Mike Alcock
for opening my eyes to the possibilities

Contents

1

Lost riches

Listen to politicians banging on about the rise in food prices and you'd think it was beyond all human control. It's to do with global demographics, climate change and economic surges they tell us. They might as well blame things on an asteroid landing in the middle of Lincolnshire and taking out half the farmland in East Anglia.

Of course, this blaming of arbitrary forces might just have something to do with the fact that, not long ago, those same politicians were assuring us that food security was no longer an issue. The great global market would provide, they told us. And for a while it seemed they were right. We got so used to food being cheap, that heaving out half the fridge contents with the rubbish became one of the weekly rituals.

Not any more. We're all taking a lot more notice of check-out prices these days. Even those who think of themselves as comfortably off are taking rather fewer trips to the farmers' market than they used to. A lot of us are getting just as adept at finding our way around Lidl as we once were in the local M&S Food Hall.

The government's had a change of heart, too. A report from the Cabinet Office's Strategy Unit conceded that Britain was a million miles away from an environmentally sustainable food chain. The penny finally seems to have dropped that a reliable supply of healthy, affordable food might just matter to Britain's political stability.[1]

To an old farming hack like me there's a certain irony in all this. For years, the only story in town was the old perennial of Europe's infamous food mountains and how to get rid of them. Right now there must be a good few Government ministers who'd happily give up half their Parliamentary majorities to see those mountains back again.

In Britain and other western countries food price inflation has outstripped almost everything else in sight, apart from oil. For families, this has added substantially to the weekly food bill, making everyone feel worse off.

In poor countries the results have been a good deal worse. Rocketing prices for rice, maize and other staples have led to shortages and hunger. We've witnessed street protests and civil disorder. I've even heard the dire predictions of Thomas Malthus trotted out by the pundits.

Malthus was the 18th century political economist who had the idea that human populations would always grow faster than their food supply. It was a grim theory. In essence it meant you could forget all your grand ideas about progress and human rights. Every social advance was destined to be brought to nothing by famine.

For someone my age – growing up under post-war food rationing – such bleak predictions had a smack of truth about them. There was even a morbid fascination, especially among teenage males fixated on sex, death and pestilence. We'd sit in our favourite coffee bar, speculating on when the inevitable food riots were likely to break out in the streets.

Then came the Cuban missile crisis. Suddenly there seemed a lot more chance we'd all get vaporised in a nuclear exchange before we hit twenty. So we gave up worrying about food shortages.

Food security has now been off the political agenda for close on half a century. What solved the problem – or so we thought – was the so-called "green revolution" of the 1960s and 70s. Clever plant breeders came up with a new family of high-yield wheat and rice strains. These varieties had short stems and went by endearing names like Hobbit. They produced gigantic harvests - just so long as you fed them with huge amounts of nitrate fertilizer.

The new varieties promised an end to hunger, at least for those countries that had the money to pay. They weren't much help to the world's poor, who continued suffering from malnutrition and famine. But across most of the planet, the green revolution kept grain plentiful and cheap - so cheap we've taken to feeding half of it to our farm animals. As an exercise in waste it must rank up there with the Caribbean stag party or taking a trip to the corner shop in a Hummer.

Now suddenly the seemingly endless flow of grain doesn't look quite so certain. Even here in the west, the idea of shortages has quietly insinuated itself back into our consciousness. It's like glimpsing an old stray dog we'd forgotten about, but which has started following us again.

International food experts responded by calling for greater global investment in agriculture. This is widely interpreted by farmers and agribusiness as a green light for more of the same – that is, more intensive grain growing. Around the world giant tractors are lumbering up and down the landscape of open skies, planting new land with wheat, rice and maize crops, then dosing them with chemical fertilizers and pesticides.

Bio-technology companies have added their siren voices to the clamour. It's as if we're back in the 1960s with the promise of a green revolution. Only now it's the wonderful, new GM crops that'll give us a golden harvest. "Trust us and we'll solve the food crisis," chorus the heads of corporate agribusiness. But we shouldn't because they can't.

Far from giving the world greater security, our present food system – based on the global trading of grains - will lead to catastrophe. It's robbing everyday foods of the health-protecting nutrients we need, while insidiously damaging our farmland so it'll be incapable of feeding future generations.

As if this weren't bad enough, it's adding to our climate change woes. Who would believe our food supply could be responsible for 18 per cent of our greenhouse gas emissions?[2] Whatever happened to our green and pleasant land?

The good news is there's an alternative – a different way of producing our food. It's a tried and tested method. No great new scientific break-throughs are required. It won't make food expensive or lead to elitist products that benefit just a fortunate few.

Quite simply it will make a whole range of everyday staple foods healthier for everyone. What's more it'll make the land richer and more fertile so it will go on producing healthy foods for our grandchildren and their children too. It will fill our countryside with wildlife and even fight climate change.

So what is this miracle system that sounds almost too good to be true? It's one we're all familiar with. It's principally what made Britain the beautiful and prosperous island it is. And if widely adopted today it would bring new life to the countryside.

It has to be said, there would be little in it for the global chemical corporations who do so well out of the current system. We'd have no need for pesticides and precious little need for chemical fertilizers. As for the bio-tech companies – who expect to make a killing from their GM seeds – they'd hardly get a look in.

Instead the profits would mostly stay in the countryside, with the farmers and their staff who grow the foods. Which could be the reason we hear so little about it. Our political leaders and the big corporations have done their best to hush up its benefits. But we can neglect it no longer. In a world of climate change and growing food insecurity we need this great natural resource more than ever before.

The last time Britain faced a threat to its food supply was during the dark days of World War Two. In the years leading up to the war more than half the nation's food was imported – wheat from north America, bacon and dairy foods from Denmark, beef from south America. With the onset of hostilities, the supply lines were disrupted by German submarines and consequently Britain was forced to rely more heavily on home production.

The famous "dig for victory" campaign urged ordinary citizens to grow food on every available patch of land including lawns, gardens and parks. Out in the countryside an even more dramatic transformation was taking place. Over the six years of war British farmers doubled their output of wheat, increasing the area planted to the crop by 82 per cent. At the same time they stepped up their cattle numbers. Despite a shortage of animal feeds – a result of the submarine blockade – our output of home-grown beef and dairy foods soared.

In the autumn of 1941, after just two years of war, Britain's great leader Winston Churchill was able to give the nation's farmers and farm workers a heart-felt pat on the back. He told them: "Never before have you responded to the country's call as you have done in the last two years. It is due in no small measure to the efforts you have made, in spite of many difficulties, that we find ourselves in a better position on the food front than at any previous time since the war started."

It's sobering to realise that today's farmers would no longer be capable of responding to such a national emergency. Without huge imports of fuel oil and energy-rich fertilizers and pesticides they couldn't maintain present levels of production, let alone produce more. What the wartime farmers had on their side was a resource seldom mentioned outside geography books.

When they answered the nation's call and ploughed up their land for wheat crops, they knew that, even without imported fertilizers, the soil would contain all the necessary plant nutrients to ensure a good crop. Their soils were highly fertile – they contained what you might call a strategic reserve of crop-growing potential. The possession of fertile soils was almost as good as having wheat safely stored in the barn.

The chief reason why Britain possessed this life-saving bank of fertility was that farmers made full use of another crop, one which had laid the foundations of the nation's wealth and prosperity centuries before. It's a crop that grows so well on this island, few of us think of it as having to be specially cultivated. This is why, over the centuries, it has made such a spectacular contribution to the health and well-being of the British people.

A few miles to the west of Cranborne Chase in Dorset stands a huge chalk outcrop known as Hambledon Hill. When its Neolithic earthworks were excavated they were found to contain large numbers of animal bones, mostly from cattle. It seems the main foods of the people occupying these chalk hills more than 4,000 years ago were wild plants and fruits together with dairy foods, pig meat and mutton. Though they ate small amounts of grain, far more important were foods from grazing animals - the foods of grassland.

This island off the northwest mainland of Europe has always grown good grass. With its maritime climate of mild, wet winters and warm summers, pastures stayed lush and green for most of the year. Through the nation's history it was grass that could be relied upon to feed the people when the grain harvest failed or when the price of bread went sky high.

An Italian visitor to Britain during the reign of Elizabeth 1 remarked of the English: "They often eat mutton and beef, which is generally considered to be better here than anywhere else in the world. This is due to the excellence of their pastures."

When the wheat harvest failed – as often happened in Tudor times – the poor went without bread. But whatever the price of bread, an acre or two of pasture would feed the peasant family's house cow, keeping them supplied with milk, butter and cheese throughout the year.

In the dark days of World War Two it was grassland that supplied our beef, milk, butter, cheese, eggs and chicken, together with much of our pork. It was this same grassland that built up the fertility of our soils so that – when the pastures were ploughed – we could grow the wheat we could no longer import from America. Our home pastures did as much to ensure Britain's survival as the Spitfire, radar, the bouncing bomb and all the other great technical achievements of wartime.

Even in the 1960s grassland remained a major producer of Britain's food. As an agricultural student I worked on large farms in Berkshire and in Dorset. Though both grew cereal crops, they also produced large quantities of food from grassland – beef, milk and lamb. These were classical mixed farms, the great British invention that fed a fast-growing population during the nation's transition to an industrial power.

As country people have known for generations, grassland provides a truly secure source of food. While cereal crops can fail, victims of drought, storm, flood and tempest, well managed grassland will survive all such natural disasters and provide a secure food supply.

Unlike cereal crops, pasture-fed foods are genuinely home-grown. To grow wheat crops farmers must buy in chemical fertilizers, pesticides and fossil fuels, most of which have to be imported. Clover-rich pastures need no inputs, not even nitrate fertilizers. They create their own fertility. And, once they're ploughed up, they bequeath that fertility to the arable crops that follow. That's how the wartime grasslands also provided the wheat for our bread.

Unlike cereal grains, the foods of grasslands don't require huge machines and the diesel fuel to run them. Pastured animals – beef cattle, dairy cows, hens, geese, even pigs – provide their own motive power. They move around at will in an environment that is wholly natural. This means they stay healthy and grow strong. No big tractors are required, no giant harvesters, no fossil fuels.

The grasses grow and the animals flourish, their manure adding to the fertility of the soil; it is a timeless and sustainable system. Well-managed pastures will go on producing healthy animal foods year after year if we need them to. Or, if we choose, we can plough the grass from time to time to grow wheat and vegetables from the accumulated fertility before sowing the land back to grass.

The foods from this land can be truly called "local". They're grown from the natural fertility of the local soil, not from imported grains or chemical fertilizer produced in the gas fields of Kazakhstan. While feed grains can be shipped anywhere in the world – wherever the price is highest – pastures are always there, always local, always producing food down the end of a British lane.

Despite these benefits we have come to rely on grains to underpin our food system. Of all the nourishing foods produced from grass until the mid 20th century, only lamb is still mainly, though not exclusively, pasture fed. Even beef and dairy foods – in nature the foods of grazing ruminant animals – are frequently produced from animals shut up in sheds and fed on cereal grains.

Where grasslands once fed the nation, our food supply now rests to a dangerous degree on wheat and other grains. That's why a crop failure in the US or Ukraine is likely to send the prices of dozens of foods spiralling in the local Tesco or Sainsbury's. When the Chinese buy up shiploads of grain to feed the cattle that will supply their multiplying burger bars, we all pay the price in our weekly shop. When we relied on grassland for our foods we were protected from such volatility.

There's another reason why we should worry about the revolution in the way we produce our basic foods. The evidence is now stacking up that foods from animals fed on large amounts of grain are less healthy than pasture-fed foods; in fact they can be downright dangerous.

Beef raised on grains, for example – which would include a good deal of British beef and almost all American beef – contains more saturated fats and lower levels of protective omega-3 fats than pasture-fed beef. And while beef produced on clover-filled grassland is rich in a powerful, cancer-fighting compound known as CLA, grain-fed beef contains almost none of it.

If grain feeding is such a dubious habit why do so many farmers do it? One reason is that for decades European Union subsidies for growing cereal crops have made them cheap. There's been good money to be had by turning them into meat or milk. Huge surpluses – subsidised by the United States as well as the EU - have flowed around the world undercutting traditional grazing methods.

Whether by design or accident, governments have made traditional grazing uneconomic. As a result many farmers have little or no knowledge of just how productive good grassland can be.

I once wrote an opinion piece for *Farmers Weekly,* the magazine that gave me my first job in journalism back in the early 1970s. In the article I set out the health and environmental benefits of raising farm livestock on pasture. The following week's issue contained a letter from a leading East Anglian cereal grower, pointing out that in his part of the country drought was not unknown, so pasture growing wasn't an option.

In fact the correspondent was mistaken in his analysis. Pasture-based production isn't merely possible under arid conditions, it's the only sustainable way of producing food. In a prolonged drought cereal growing is only possible with the help of irrigation, which adds to the already substantial fossil energy load of this form of farming. A mixed species pasture containing deep-rooting herbs will go on growing long after cereal crops have given up the struggle.

If climate change is going to give us drier summers, as many experts predict, we'll need to rely more on our pastures just to keep ourselves fed.

There's no better example of the productive power of pastures than the great prairie grasslands of America before the European settlers arrived. Under its original, semi-natural grassland, the region known as The Great Plains – the arid heartland of America stretching from the Mississippi to the Rockies – supported more than fifty million bison. Over the centuries, the prairie grasses maintained vast nomadic herds through periods of drought, fire and storm.

Then came the railroads, bringing with them the sharp-shooters who killed the bison and made war on native Americans. They were followed by the dirt-farmers with their barbed wire, steel ploughs and dreams of waving wheat.

Today the grasslands, the bison and the native Americans have gone. The plains are under intensive arable crops, mainly wheat, corn and soya beans. Most of these grains are fed to cattle, or at least they were until George Bush introduced subsidies for biofuel production. Until then the expensively-grown crops fed about forty-five million cattle. But growing them required irrigation, public subsidies and huge amounts of chemical fertilizer, pesticides and fossil fuel, all to replace the bison that required none of these.

In the words of Richard Manning, author of a classic book on the American prairies: "A century's worth of work, warfare and technology replaced fifty million bison with forty-five million cattle whose meat is fattier and higher in cholesterol. One wonders what progress is for."[3]

Here in Britain we managed to destroy our grasslands as effectively as the Americans did theirs, though in a less spectacular way. Though many were ploughed up in the scramble to grow cereals, most were simply ruined by neglect.

At the end of World War Two a political consensus emerged that farmers, who had helped to feed the nation during hostilities, should not be abandoned with the coming of peace. However, there was no clear agreement about what sort of agriculture the country needed.

A group of influential scientists led by the charismatic George Stapledon urged that Britain's food production should be based on grassland. During the war thousands of acres of pasture-land had been ploughed up to grow wheat. Now Stapledon wanted the nation to return to grass, her first and greatest source of wealth.

Before the war Stapledon and his team at the Welsh Plant Breeding Station in Aberystwyth had bred a new family of productive grass varieties to replace the poor quality seed then being sold by merchants. He wanted these new varieties used to re-vitalise the productivity of hill farms. He urged the country to return to traditional mixed farming, the rotation of cereal crops and short-term grass "leys" over the same land.

With the support of cash from taxpayers, mixed farming based on grass leys spread rapidly across lowland Britain. At the height of the ley farming boom in the early 1960s, the area of land under "temporary" grass leys was double what it had been during the depression years before the war.

Stapledon intended his grassland revolution to give the nation healthy foods while at the same time bringing economic revival to the countryside. He dreamed of a prosperous countryside – revitalised by a thriving agriculture – and supporting a growing population. To him the land was a great unifying factor in national life.

Sadly his utopian dreams were to be dashed. The growing productivity of agriculture led, not to the thriving community of small farms he had hoped for, but to the emergence of large predatory holdings which began swallowing up their smaller neighbours.

The subsidy system produced specialist farms, particularly large-scale arable holdings. Many farmers found it more profitable to get rid of grass from the rotation and concentrate on growing cereal crops. Without the fertility-building benefits of grass they would be reliant on chemical fertilizers and sprays to grow decent crops, but generous payments from the taxpayer were more than enough to cover these extra costs.

The principal problem for the new cereal growers was how to prevent the price of this swelling tide of grain dropping through the floor. There was an obvious solution. They could add value by feeding it to livestock – effectively converting grain into meat. It was a development that was to strike a devastating blow to the nation's health.

As a student in the 1960s I once went to visit one of these prototype "factory farms". It produced what the farming press innocently called "barley beef". To me it seemed a miserable sort of operation – a hundred or so young cattle cooped up in the half-light of a large shed. They stood on concrete slats munching on their diet of grains. Never would they walk on the green turf for which evolution had prepared them.

The farmer seemed enthusiastic enough. As far as he was concerned, this was the future of beef production – fast, efficient and easily mechanised. What no one understood at the time was how unhealthy this kind of meat would be when compared with the meat of animals grazing naturally on clover-rich pasture.

While few British farmers now house their cattle all year round, many feed them large amounts of unhealthy grains in place of grass. Poultry and pigs are often kept in confinement. Unless they are officially labelled as "free range", almost all chicken, eggs, pork and bacon are from animals kept in confinement and fed mainly on grains.

While these factory methods can produce large amounts of cheap protein and fat, they are "dumbed down" foods, depleted of many health-protecting nutrients that grassland once put there. As Britain - along with other western industrial countries – battles with an epidemic of degenerative diseases, it's clear that much of it can be attributed to poor food.

According to the Cabinet Office Strategy Unit report, ill health caused by diet costs the National Health Service an extra £6 billion a year.

In his book *The Way of the Land*, George Stapledon warned that the abandonment of grassland and mixed farming would lead ultimately to disaster.[4] The nation has never needed his pastoral revolution more than now.

Just as it improves human health, grassland farming can do much to restore the health of the planet. Intensive crop farming relies heavily on chemical fertilizers which are the biggest source of carbon emissions in agriculture. They are the major producer of nitrous oxide, which as a greenhouse gas is far more damaging than carbon dioxide.

Established grassland, containing clovers and deep-rooting herbs, needs none of these polluting inputs to produce good food. Compared with modern industrial crops, grasslands have deeper root systems that enable them to take up more nutrients from the soil. Although farmers use chemical fertilizers on grassland, they'd have no need of them if they got the management right.

Grasslands hold another ace card in the battle against climate change – their ability to boost the level of carbon stored in the soil. All soils contain carbon in the form of organic matter, which can be made up from both living organisms and decaying plant and animal residues. The level of carbon as organic matter can play a part in the regulation of carbon in the atmosphere.

A fertile soil can easily contain 10 per cent or more of its mass as organic matter in the top thirty centimetres or so. This amounts to around four hundred tonnes of soil organic matter in every hectare of land. But cultivation – together with the battery of fertilizers and pesticides used by crop growers – steadily reduces the level of organic matter, releasing ever more carbon into the atmosphere.

Many soils under continuous cultivation for wheat and other crops now contain less than 1 per cent as organic matter, amounting to just forty tonnes of organic matter per hectare. The carbon contained in this "lost" organic material hasn't simply disappeared. It has been added to the atmospheric load of greenhouse gases, hastening climate change.

By contrast grasslands build up soil organic matter, taking carbon from the atmosphere and locking it away below ground. A team of British scientists established this more than twenty years ago, though their findings have largely been ignored by policy-makers. In the early 1950s – when Britain had scarcely shrugged off wartime rationing – a team of researchers embarked on a thirty-year experiment to compare the sustainability of producing food from grassland and from cultivated crops.[5]

The researchers, from the now-defunct Grassland Research Institute in Berkshire, looked at soil conditions under grazed pasture and under farmland cultivated every year for arable crops.

At the end of the experiment the organic matter content of the intensively-cropped soil had fallen by a third, even though it had been at a low level to start with. The soil now contained little more than 1 per cent organic matter. The upper soil layers had become so hard that any crops they grew were highly susceptible to drought. Without their annual fix of chemicals they'd have been incapable of producing anything.

However, the soil under pasture showed a steady rise in fertility. A huge population of earthworms showed that it was in a far healthier state than the cultivated land. What's more, the organic matter levels in the soil had risen by more than half in the first ten years, equivalent to an annual increase of more than a tonne of soil carbon to every hectare.

It's one of the extraordinary gifts of grasslands that, even as they produce more food, the fertility of their soils increases so they have the potential to produce even more. As if this weren't glorious enough, the nutrient content of those foods grows too. Year by year carefully-managed pasture farms turn out more food and healthier food, at the same time enriching the soil and safeguarding the food supply in years to come. Grass comes as close as anything could to delivering the elusive "free lunch".

If there's a downside, it lies in the management skills needed to make the whole thing work. As we'll see later in this book, running an efficient grazing system is both an art and a science. It's a skill once common but now rare, even in farming communities. By contrast, chemical grain growing is easy. It's just a matter of getting the routine operations done at the right time.

Only now are scientists beginning to unravel the reasons for the wonderful efficiency of grassland farming. The cultivated crops we grow for ourselves and our food animals are all annual plants –

they have to be grown afresh from seed every year. Their root systems don't have time to grow to any great depth. This is why modern crops need such heavy inputs of chemical fertilizers.

However grasslands contain mostly perennial plants that continue to grow year after year. Their roots can go down to great depths, sometimes several metres. Many form symbiotic links with a group of soil fungi called arbuscular mycorrhizae. It's these fungi that help build up the stores of soil carbon. That's what makes grassland soils so fertile and so beneficial in regulating atmospheric carbon. Not only do they offer food security, they could – if we chose to use them - save the planet.

Today, ruminant animals such as cattle and sheep get a lot of flack from environmentalists because microbial action in the rumen, the animal's fermentation chamber, produces large amounts of the hydrocarbon gas methane. This is a damaging greenhouse gas, twenty-three times more powerful than carbon dioxide. For this reason, dairy foods and the meat of cattle and sheep are said to be harmful to the planet. But the argument doesn't stand close scrutiny. As we shall see later, a number of plants found in species-rich, natural grasslands are known to reduce methane emissions.

More important, ruminants raised by traditional, pasture-based methods are part of a system that locks up vast amounts of carbon in the soil. The net effect is hugely beneficial in the fight against climate change, even allowing for methane emissions. It's the feeding of grain to animals that's damaging to the planet, not the production of healthy foods on traditional pastoral systems.

In view of the mounting threat to our environment, continuing the production of cereals and other grains for feeding to animals is an extravagance we can no longer afford. Intensive crop growing – with all its chemical inputs and environmental damage – might have had short-term advantages when oil was plentiful and cheap, and when governments were handing out generous farm subsidies. Today the political tide has turned against subsidies and the price of oil price has reached new heights. On cost grounds alone we need a new approach.

Recent events in commodity markets may bring about a return to pasture farming far quicker than any of us predicted. The habit of feeding cereals, maize and soya to animals was based on a plentiful supply of cheap grains. They made the healthier alternative of pasture farming uneconomic.

Today the cheap grains aren't around. Growing demand from China and India has helped send prices soaring. American and European Union subsidies on biofuel production have pushed them even higher. Fertilizer and pesticide prices have followed the oil price upwards. Suddenly the feeding of grain to animals isn't looking so attractive any more. Britain now needs a cheaper, more secure food supply.

Against this the persuasive voices of global agribusiness continue to portray pasture farming and other low-input systems as "backward" and "unscientific" – a sort of sentimental longing for a lost golden age. It's a transparent attempt to distort popular understanding of what real food is. But it seems to be having an impact.

A *Times* columnist took western countries to task for turning their backs on high-tech, disease-free, weed-resistant crops in favour of "medieval organic farming practices that involve persuading your pets to poop more so that you'll have something nourishing to sprinkle on your allotment".[6]

What's new and modern has always held a fascination for people. Agribusiness companies exploit this natural urge for advancement. They perpetuate the myth that natural systems are unproductive and new technologies are always better. Cut through the corporate propaganda and you'll find the opposite is the case. When they're allowed to, natural processes almost always outperform the industrial model.

There's certainly nothing unscientific about pasture farming. Any rational appraisal will show that it can produce a wide range of benefits – a clean environment, flood protection, biodiversity, food security and climate stability.

Perhaps its greatest gift is health. If we're going to eat dairy foods and meat, it's worth making sure they were raised on pasture. Later in this book we'll explore how to find them. But first let's take an unsentimental look at what it is that makes pasture-fed foods so good for you.

2

How grass keeps you healthy

My earliest food memories date back to when we lived in my grand parents' Reading council house during the years of scarcity that followed World War Two. Though no one had any money to speak of, we seemed to eat pretty well despite food rationing, and it's no coincidence that a fair number of our main dietary items were the foods of grassland.

Beef appeared regularly on the table. We had it roast on Sunday, cold sliced on Monday and minced in cottage pie on Tuesday. All our beef came from the Co-op butcher at the top of the road, and much of theirs was sourced in Argentina.

It would have been produced on the pampas, the great prairie grasslands that stretched from the River Plate in the north to Bahia Blanca in the south, and west to the very foothills of the Andes.

Then, as now, Argentina produced some of the world's finest beef.

Our butter came from another great grassland region, New Zealand's famous Canterbury Plains. There the pastures – with their rich mix of grasses, herbs and fertility building clovers – were grazed all year round, making the milk and butter that came from them genuinely free-range.

From time to time lamb would appear on the table. Some of this would also have come from New Zealand, with the rest from our local pastures in Berkshire. Either way it's a safe bet that it would have been entirely pasture-raised.

The one food I knew for certain to be local was our milk. Each morning the milkman delivered three pints of "silver top", the badge that declared it to be the ordinary stuff as opposed to the higher fat "gold top", the product of Jersey and Guernsey cows. Even though it had a lower fat content the thick band of yellow cream stretched a good way down the bottle. In those days skimmed and semi-skimmed milk were practically unheard of.

Our milk came from a local dairy that had been set up by a Berkshire farmer before the war. Like many dairy farmers of the inter-war period, he had been so incensed by the low prices paid by the big dairies that he started up his own milk round. By the time my brother and I had arrived to squabble over who got "the top of the milk" on his breakfast porridge, this enterprising farmer was supplying half the town.

While I've no idea how that dairy herd was run, it's a fair bet the cows would have spent a lot more time grazing fresh pasture than most herds today.

In those days there were many other foods from grass. Some

of the eggs my mother bought from the Co-op may have come from hens in mobile houses moved regularly across a grass field somewhere, allowing the birds constant access to fresh pasture. Even our Christmas pork is likely to have come from outdoor pigs rootling around in the turf.

With the memory of wartime shortages still fresh in people's minds, the foods we ate were principally the foods of grassland. The idea that animals should be fed large amounts of grain would have seemed scandalous. Not many years earlier, when U-boat packs hunted the Atlantic seaways, thousands of merchant seamen died bringing in the wheat that would produce our basic ration of bread. Fed to cattle it takes about 8kg of cereals to produce just a kilo of beef. Raising meat this way would have looked like a criminal waste of good food and an insult to the sailors who had given their lives on the convoys.

Besides, most people were perfectly happy with their everyday foods. Apart from wartime horrors such as dried egg, most foods tasted pretty much as we wanted them to taste. And unlike today, when many people are confused about which foods are good for them and which aren't, everyone considered their ordinary staples to be healthy and nourishing.

There would seem to have been good grounds for their confidence. Though the national diet was higher in saturated fat than today, levels of heart disease and cancer were far lower. For years animal fats have been demonised as the cause of many modern degenerative illnesses. Yet despite the rise of the low-fat diet, heart disease and cancer rates continue obdurately upwards. Could it be that it's not our traditional foods that are the root cause of illness, but the way we produce them, particularly the modern farming obsession for stuffing grain into animals that in the past were grazed on pasture?

The medical evidence is now stacking up that pasture-fed foods provide a range of health benefits when compared with foods from grain-fed animals. For a start, meat produced from grazing animals usually contains a lot less fat than animals shut up in yards and fed on cereal grains. Grass-fed beef, for example, contains just a quarter of the fat of grain-fed beef.

At the same time nutrient levels are far higher. Cattle grazing pastures incorporate up to ten times more beta-carotene and up to five times more vitamin E into their muscle tissues than grain-fed animals. Beta-carotene, which is converted to vitamin A in the liver, and vitamin E are fat-soluble vitamins. Both are essential nutrients vital for health.

Dairy cows grazing fresh young grass produce milk with high levels of the fat-soluble vitamins A, D, K and E. Butter made from this milk is a particularly rich source. The American dentist-turned nutritionist Weston A. Price was convinced these compounds were important in protecting against heart disease. He carried out a study of deaths from heart attacks at hospitals in different parts of the United States. He found that deaths were inversely proportional to the vitamin content of butter. When vitamin levels in butter were high – mainly in spring and autumn when cows were able to graze fast-growing pastures – death rates were low. But when vitamin levels in the butter were low – in winter and during the dry summer period – heart disease death rates shot up.[1]

Today many health experts ignore the role of fat-soluble vitamins in preventing heart attacks, mainly because they're in animal fats. And in current medical orthodoxy these are deemed to be unhealthy. Yet it has long been known that fat-soluble vitamins protect against heart disease, cancer and infections. It seems scarcely credible that foods containing them should be unhealthy, particularly when they're produced the traditional way – from grass.

Lambs grazed on pasture are also rich in fat soluble vitamins. The level of vitamin E, in particular, is far higher in the meat of pasture-fed lambs. Remarkably, vitamin levels are higher still in lambs grazed on pastures rich in wild plants. Bristol University scientists compared the nutritional quality of lambs grazing on three different types of grassland – high moorland, salt marsh and heather moorland. All three pasture-types produced lambs with higher vitamin E levels than ordinary farm grassland. The figure for lambs raised on heather moorland was spectacularly high.

It's not only vitamin levels that are raised by pasture feeding. Pastures also boost the level of health-protecting fats, particularly those known as omega-3s. These vital fats play a key role in human metabolism. New research suggests that the elimination of pasture-fed meat and milk from our diets may have been a factor in the rise in most modern degenerative diseases, including cancer, obesity, Type-2 diabetes, heart disease, autism, depression, schizophrenia and Alzheimer's. Putting these foods back in the national diet may help defeat most modern day scourges.

Omega-3s belong to a group of nutrients called essential fatty acids, so called because the body can't make them. They have to be supplied in the diet along with another related fat known as omega-6. While both types are needed by the body in small amounts, what's important is that they occur in the diet in roughly equal proportions. If one of them is consumed in far greater amounts than the other, things start to go seriously wrong.

Over the past few decades the proportion of omega-6 fats in western diets has increased dramatically while the level of omega-3s has slumped. This is because we've all been advised by nutrition experts to replace animal fats such as butter and lard with vegetable oils. Traditionally animal fats came from livestock grazing pasture, so they were rich in omega-3s. Many of the vegetable oils we've replaced them with are high in omega-6 fats. This fundamental change in the proportions of the two fats may have set people in western industrial societies on a path to disease.

Inside the body both types of fat are incorporated into the membrane of every cell. Cell membranes play a crucial part in metabolism. Not only do they control the flow of materials in and out of the cell, but they also determine the activity of enzymes and of cell messengers known as prostaglandins, which regulate a wide variety of body functions.

Within the cell membrane omega-3s and omega-6s are largely interchangeable – evolution has made them this way. In nature omega-3 fats are chiefly found in green plants and grasses, while omega-6s are found mostly in seeds. For man the hunter-gather, summer-time diets were higher in omega-3s, with omega-6s becoming more plentiful in the autumn.

According to Susan Allport, author of *The Queen of Fats*, this cyclical change in the occurrence of the two fats helps prepare humans for the season ahead. When cell membranes contain useful amounts of omega-3s, metabolism is rapid and the body is prepared for activity and reproduction. When seeds are abundant, more omega-6s are incorporated into the structure of cell membranes, and enzyme activity slows down.

As Susan Allport puts it, the body "hunkers down", getting ready for harder times to come. This means laying down extra fat to help the human animal survive through the tough winter period. Unfortunately, with modern western diets, most of us get this seasonal fat ration – with its heavy omega-6 overload – all year round. This is why we feel sluggish and have a tendency to obesity.

But the surfeit of omega-6s has an even more damaging effect on health. Prostaglandins, the cell messengers, are made from polyunsaturated fats in the cell membrane. Those made from omega-6s are more likely to produce an inflammatory response in tissues than those made from omega-3s. In small amounts omega-6 fats are a vital part of the immune system. But when there are too many of them – as in people on today's western diet – they can be the cause of heart disease, diabetes and a host of other degenerative conditions.

Susan Allport explains: "There's hardly a chronic disease of western nations that isn't linked to the double affects of these two families of fatty acids. We're talking about every cell in the body and the fact that these fatty acids wind up in the membrane of every cell. This is why almost every day you see a new disease being linked to this imbalance."[2]

Healthy diets contain roughly equal proportions of the two families so they're taken up in similar amounts for incorporation into cell membranes. In societies with long life spans – such as those in Japan and in some Mediterranean countries – cell membranes are usually found to contain omega-3s and omega-6s in balanced amounts, allowing for the normal seasonal variations.

People on modern western diets, with a high content of omega-6s, need to find rich sources of omega-3s to restore the balance. This is why they're sometimes advised to eat large amounts of fish. This isn't necessarily a good idea, particularly for pregnant women. Fish often contain heavy metals and other contaminants, so the consumption of more than one or two portions a week isn't recommended.

A better strategy for a healthy balance of fats would be to cut back on vegetable oils – together with the processed foods that often contain them – and to replace them with traditional fats such as butter. So long as it's from the milk of animals on a mainly pasture diet, it'll supply the omega-3s you need.

Omega-3s are linked to photosynthesis and are formed in the green leaves of plants and in ocean plankton. This is why seafoods are a rich source. But they are also found in useful amounts in the meat of grass-fed animals. When these animals are taken off pasture and transferred to grain-based diets, the level of omega-3s falls quickly.

Cattle and sheep fed mainly on fresh grass have been found to produce meat with up to two-thirds more omega-3 fatty acids than animals fed grain-based diets. It's the same for milk. Dairy cows grazing on fresh grass produce milk with higher levels of omega-3s. Research at Aberdeen University showed that the levels of omega-3s were, on average, 30 per cent higher in organic milk than in conventionally-produced milk.[3] However, the differences were greatest in the summer months when the organically farmed cows had access to fresh grass and clover-rich pastures.

What seems to matter is how much fresh grass there is in the animal's diet, whether or not the diet is organic. Omega-3 levels in organic milk are generally higher because under the rules organic farmers must supply at least 60 per cent of the cow's diet in the form of grass or forage. But forage can include fermented grass or silage, a feed producing far fewer omega-3s than fresh pasture. That's why – organic or not - farmers running their herds on pasture for much of the year are likely to produce the best milk, at least in terms of these health-protecting fats.

Omega-3s are not the only health protector grasslands have to offer those who eat meat and dairy foods. Conjugated linoleic acid, known as CLA, is an omega-6 fatty acid with powerful health-promoting properties. It was discovered almost by accident by researchers at the University of Wisconsin. They had been studying various foods looking for cancer-causing compounds produced by cooking. Instead they found CLA which is now known to be an effective cancer fighter. It has also been shown to protect against heart disease, diabetes and obesity. The compound is present in large amounts in the meat and milk of animals grazing fresh pasture, but when even small amounts of grain are introduced into the diet the levels in food drop dramatically. In an investigation into levels in milk, cows getting their entire ration from grazing pasture were found to produce milk with five times more CLA than cows on conventional, grain-based rations.[4]

The more lush the pasture, the greater the amount of this health-promoting compound that ends up in the meat or milk. On average the fat of Irish milk contains up to three times more CLA than the fat of American milk, which is mostly produced from housed cattle fed on grains.[5]

Even modest amounts of CLA can have a big impact on health. One researcher estimated that eating a single serving of grass-fed meat a day – plus a portion of cheese and a glass of milk from a grass-fed cow – can significantly reduce the risk of cancer.[6]

Most dairy foods made from the milk of grazing ruminants contain high levels of CLA. This includes butter, yogurts and many types of cheese. Beef, lamb and other meats from grazing ruminant animals are also rich in the compound. Even grazing turkeys are able to produce the compound from fatty acids in their diet.

For generations the people of Britain have eaten everyday foods that protected them against heart disease, cancer and a variety of other degenerative diseases. But because of changes in the way we raise our farm animals – especially ruminants like cattle and sheep – few consumers now get the levels of protection they need.

While all pastures put CLA into the meat and milk of grazing animals, traditional, herb-rich pastures produce the best results. This is because CLA is produced in the animal's rumen by the action of microbes on a simpler substance called alpha-linoleic acid, found in the leaves of plants. While grasses contain good levels of the compound, it occurs in much larger amounts in the leaves of wild plants such as dandelion, knapweed, cat's-ear, ox-eye daisy, plantain, rough hawkbit, self-heal, bird's-foot trefoil, clover, sorrel and yarrow.

A century ago almost all Britain's grasslands contained this rich diversity of wild species. It was these flower-filled pastures that inspired generations of poets and artists. Today most have gone, victims of the modern farming fashion for "clean" grassland and the chemical fertilizers and sprays that produce it.

The last time I saw pasture fields like this was on a walking holiday in the Jura – the French side of the limestone plateau that runs parallel to the Alps. Wherever we went, the pastures seemed to be full of herbs and wild flowers, and I don't just mean the rough hill pastures. We saw plenty of species-rich grasslands like this in the more fertile fields close to the smartly-maintained farmhouses.

Quite a few of the plants I recognised. I spotted yarrow, plantain, silverweed, vetch, dandelion, bird's-foot trefoil, hawkweed, clovers – both red and white, scabious and gentian. Along with these familiar plants were a number of others I didn't know. They obviously weren't in the pastures by accident. They'd been sown deliberately. And it didn't take us long to find out why.

This was the home region of Comte cheese, considered by a foodie friend of mine to be one of finest cheeses in the world. We ate a lot of it on that holiday. It has a sweet, nutty taste with lingering flavours that give it real depth. In the French Jura you see it everywhere – from cafes and truck-stops to the top hotels *gastronomique*.

The rules for producing it are strict, and they start right there on the farm. Milk producers are not allowed to use nitrate fertilizers, nor are they permitted to feed their red-and-white cows any fermented feeds - which means silage is out. The cows are virtually free-range – they stay out on the pastures for much of the year. The farmers don't even bring them in for milking. They milk them in the fields through mobile milking parlours called bails. Back in the early 20th century these were widely used in parts of Britain, particularly on the southern chalk downlands and on the low-lying pastures of the Somerset Levels.

In the Jura dairy farmers have stuck with pasture farming because, despite the cheap grain that has been knocking about in the EU (at least until 2007), grazing produces a superb-tasting cheese that everyone wants to buy. And though the cheese connoisseurs might not realise it, the chances are they're getting a life-extending dose of CLA. Could this be one of the reasons why the French live so long?

I got the chance of a chat with one of the local farmers in the bar of a small hotel where we stayed one night. In the best French I could muster, I asked him if he'd ever thought of boosting his milk output by feeding his cows on grain and soya as many British farmers do. He looked at me as if I needed locking up.

"Why would I want to make an industrial cheese," he retorted, "when I can do very nicely producing real food. This way our customers are happy, we're happy and the tourist office is happy. And in case you haven't noticed, the cows are happy, too."

As it happens I had noticed. Coming from the UK it was difficult not to. Back at home we're used to seeing the overworked black-and-white Holstein cow, bony, tired-looking and often lame. By contrast these Jura cows – the breed is Montbeliard, we discovered – appeared sturdy, bright-eyed and alert. It's another reason why it's better to eat the meat and dairy foods of grass-fed animals rather than the produce of grain-fed cattle.

Feeding large amounts of grain to ruminant animals like cattle makes their digestive systems abnormally acidic. This can lead to lameness, infertility and udder infections. All these conditions are rife in today's dairy industry. There are dangers for consumers, too. Grain feeding of cattle greatly increases the risk from dangerous pathogens such as *E. coli* strain 0157.

It takes as few as ten of these organisms to cause illness, even death in human beings. In the highly acidic conditions of grain-fed cattle the bacteria develop a degree of acid tolerance. This makes them more hazardous to humans, since they're able to withstand the acid conditions of our own digestive systems.

Scientists at Cornell University found that when cattle on a grain-rich diet were switched to a grass-based diet, their production of acid-resistant *E. coli* bacteria dropped substantially after just a few days.[7] Ruminants on their natural diet of fresh pasture stay healthy so the foods they produce are not only richer in nutrients, but safer. Just how safe has been investigated on a pioneering dairy farm in California.

In the fertile San Joaquin Valley near Fresno, farmer Mark McAfee produces pasture-fed milk for a growing band of enthusiasts, particularly a group he calls "passionate moms". These are mothers who have discovered, that not only is grass-fed milk best for their children, but that to gain the maximum nutritional benefit they need to drink it raw and unpasteurized. They've found that when children replace commercial milk with pasture-fed, raw milk, their asthma disappears or their allergies improve.

The family-owned dairy farm, known as Organic Pastures Dairy Company, (OPDC), started selling raw milk in January, 2002.[8] The milk is now sold in stores throughout California as well as to health-conscious consumers in all 50 US states.

To meet California's strict safety standards for the sale of raw milk, OPDC milk must contain fewer than 15,000 bacteria per ml. Though the state's food and agriculture department regularly samples the milk, McAfee carries out his own tests on every batch, posting the results daily on the farm's website. The average bacteria count currently stands at just 2,285. In Britain dairy farmers are allowed to market milk with up to 100,000 bacteria per ml, though it has to be pasteurized.

Neither the state authorities nor the farm's own tests have ever found a pathogen in Mark McAfee's milk. The state authorities test for three human pathogens: *Listeria monocytogenes*, *Salmonella* and *E. coli 0157*. In more than five years of intensive testing not a single pathogen has been detected.

In experiments carried out by the University of California, dung from OPDC cows was found to contain no trace of salmonella, even though human pathogens have been found on 30 per cent of conventional farms. McAfee is convinced that the combination of grass feeding and the absence of antibiotics and hormones – together with low levels of grain in the diet – change the cows' immune and digestive systems, preventing the development and spread of pathogens.

It's not just cattle and sheep that deliver a health bonus from pasture feeding. Virtually all food animals benefit from regular access to fresh grassland. Eggs from pasture-raised hens provide an array of health-protecting nutrients. Compared with the eggs of caged, grain fed birds, genuinely free-range eggs contain higher levels of B vitamins, particularly folic acid and vitamin B12, and considerably more omega-3 fatty acids plus higher levels of vitamins A and E.

Free-range birds are also less likely to be infected with *salmonella*, the bacterium responsible for most cases of food poisoning. A UK survey showed that no fewer than a quarter of farms with caged birds tested positive for salmonella. In free-range flocks fewer than 7 per cent of farms tested positive, while in organic flocks the figure was below 5 per cent.

The benefits of pasture-feeding apply as much to table birds as they do to egg layers. Birds raised on fresh grassland contain more B vitamins, more carotenes (especially lutein and zeaxanthine) - and more omega-3s than intensive broiler chickens. What's more, exposure to the sun ensures their fat will be richer in vitamin D. The more yellow the fat the more nutritious it'll be.

In their TV shows, both Hugh Fearnley-Whittingstall and Jamie Oliver urged viewers to pay a little more for their chicken and to buy only free-range birds. In doing so the chefs claimed that consumers would help put an end to the inhumane conditions under which caged birds were raised. They might have added – but didn't – that an end to these conditions would be as good for consumers as for the wretched factory chickens. Freeing the birds would lead to a healthier life for people.

However, the full nutritional and health benefits apply only to pasture-raised poultry. When it comes to chicken the term "free range" is much abused. It can mean simply allowing birds onto the same piece of soiled, pecked-over grassland day after day. This will do little either for the health of the birds or for the health of the people who consume them.

Chicken manure is high in nitrogen. If there's any grass left on the over-stocked patch of land, the manure produces a bitter-tasting forage that the birds don't want to eat. Moving the chickens' mobile house to a new patch of fresh grass at regular intervals keeps the ground clean and gives the birds continuous access to nutritious, leafy greens.

If anything, the benefits of pasture for turkeys are even greater than for chickens, mainly because they forage over a wider area. They thrive on green plants and insects in the pasture, producing meat which, unlike chicken, is high in cancer-fighting CLA.

According to Virginia grass farmer Joel Salatin, turkeys will get up to half their feed off pasture, compared with only 15 per cent or so with chickens. Adult turkeys can also withstand harsh weather better than chickens. They are, quite simply, "the most nutritious, best tasting birds in the world," he says.[9]

Even pigmeat is healthier when it's from animals reared on pasture rather than shut in sheds and fed mostly on grain. Sows raised on grassland have more vitamin E and selenium, (a powerful anti-oxidant), in their milk than grain-fed animals. These higher levels of nutrients appear in the meat too.

What all this evidence adds up to is that moving farm animals from their traditional grazings into sheds has had a deleterious effect on our health. The unintended consequence has been to rob diets of health-protecting nutrients and fuel the near epidemic of obesity and degenerative diseases in western industrial nations.

Not even an organic label guarantees that we're getting our full measure of the pasture-fed nutrients our bodies need. The choice of organically-grown foods can ensure that what we eat is free of pesticide residues, GM crops and synthetic hormones. But it provides no assurance that a food is produced mainly on grassland, so it won't help us maximise the level of omega-3s or CLA in our diets.

For example, some organic dairy foods may well be made from the milk of cows that spend long periods grazing fresh grass. But others will contain the milk of cows fed to the minimum organic standards, with their requirement for 60 per cent of the ration to be in the form of forage – fibrous foods – including silage. The difference in nutrient content could be substantial.

The same applies to beef and other meats. The healthiest are likely to come from animals raised on pasture, particularly pastures with a rich mix of plant species. An organic label may be a helpful guide. In some cases it will identify foods from animals fed mainly on fresh grass. Certainly it will exclude permanently housed and intensively grain-fed animals. But there are many fine foods from largely pastured animals that won't have an organic label.

Finding these foods in modern supermarkets isn't easy. A traditional favourite is Anchor butter, made in New Zealand from pasture-fed cows. Most of today's butter – including many premium brands – is made from the milk of cows fed considerable amounts of grain, maize silage and soya.

My local branch of Tesco sometimes stocks organic beef from Argentina. This is almost certain to be grass-fed. It's not that I'm particularly happy buying imported foods, far from it. If I knew of locally-produced versions I'd go for them every time. But an animal's grazing history rarely gets a mention on food labels, so it's not easy finding the best foods even when they're on the shelf.

What it means is there's no real alternative to asking questions of the retailer – the store manager or the stall-holder. As the health benefits of pasture feeding become better known, this aspect of the production process is likely to feature more often on the label.

Fortunately, I know of a number of beef farmers who raise cattle almost entirely on pasture. One of them lives a few miles from my home on Exmoor. He breeds pedigree Devon cattle on the eastern fringes of the moor. All year round he runs his herd on unfertilised, flower-filled pastures until they're ready to go to the butcher. That's about the sum total of his production system. It's about as simple as it could be – just grass. It also happens to produce some of the healthiest meat around.

A few years ago most beef was produced this way. Then in the 1960s and 70s - when cheap grain became plentiful – farmers got rid of their traditional grassland breeds like the Devon or Red Ruby. Most farmers replaced them with more fashionable Continental breeds such as the Charolais – breeds that would put on weight quickly on a diet high in grain, giving the farmer a speedy return and the abattoir a big margin.

Thankfully my beef farmer friend stuck with his beloved Devons and the simple pasture system he believed in, despite some gentle ribbing from his farming neighbours. But he's had the last laugh. Customers now travel from near and far to stock their freezers with his superlative meat.

Today many of these traditional animal foods seem to come with a health warning. Their fats are considered harmful. But the evidence is growing that, so long as the animals are mainly pasture fed, their fats actually protect health. They contain fewer calories and a lower proportion of saturated fats than those of animals on grain-based rations. Equally important, they supply more omega-3 fatty acids and CLA.

Today the best advice for living a healthy life is to forget the skimmed milk, the refined vegetable oils and the low-fat spreads promoted by the food manufacturing companies. Stick instead to the traditional foods of the countryside. Just make sure they're from animals that live their lives on grass.

By happy coincidence these aren't just the foods that'll make us healthy. There's every chance they'll stop the planet getting sick, too.

3

No more climate change

Our food supply hides a big, fat, life-denying secret. It's something no one in the food and farming business ever wants to talk about. Yet it has the potential to transform the lives of everyone on this planet as well as the lives of future generations. It's the power of soils to take carbon dioxide out of the atmosphere and to end for all time the threat of global warming.

Though you'll seldom hear it mentioned, the world's soils are the largest terrestrial reservoir of carbon. They hold three times as much of it as the atmosphere and over four times as much as vegetation.[1] On farmland, what determines whether soils take up carbon or emit it to the atmosphere is the way farmers manage their crops.

A sizeable part of the damaging extra load of greenhouse gases in the atmosphere today comes - not only from the burning of fossil fuels – but from soil carbon released when we switched from traditional farming methods to intensive grain growing.

The good news is it's a process we could easily reverse. By moving to sustainable ways of growing our food – particularly through the use of grazing animals – we could quickly put the excess carbon safely back in the soil.

In fact it would be ridiculously easy to achieve. No technical breakthroughs are required. No fancy systems for pumping carbon dioxide back into spent oil wells. Simply making sure our meat and dairy foods came from pasture-fed rather than grain-fed animals would do it.

Not only would we enjoy healthier foods, we'd be going a long way to averting climate catastrophe. The fact that such a simple solution hardly gets an airing is a measure of the powerful interests currently served by today's global grain trade.

The gaping flaw in our food supply, the one that has been so damaging to our world, is that it's based overwhelmingly on annual plants. These are plants that go through their entire life cycle in a single year. Perennials, by contrast, live for two years or more.

The difference isn't an arcane matter of interest only to botanists. It's what makes our food and its production unhealthy for the planet and ultimately, hazardous to us, the consumers.

Today's top ten food crops are all annuals. Together they occupy no less than 80 per cent of the world's cultivated land. The top three, wheat, rice and maize, account for more than half the cultivated area. The rest is sown to a variety of cereal grains, oilseeds and legumes. They include barley, sorghum, soyabeans, millet and rapeseed.

The weakness of annual species as food crops is that they must be grown from seed every year. It's the grain we're after, but to produce it the plant must first develop a mass of roots, stems and leaves before it even starts on the bit that matters. To get a crop to this stage takes massive amounts of oil energy in the form of nitrate fertilizer, pesticides, diesel fuel and heavy machinery.

Perennial crops, by contrast, hit the ground running. Once they're established, their extensive root systems survive from year to year. So when the soil warms up in spring they're able to get off to a flying start. Fully-grown root systems are much more efficient than the developing roots of annuals in pulling up water and nutrients from deep down in the soil. As a result they stay healthier and need far fewer fertilizers and pesticides.

Traditional, species-rich grasslands are made up mostly of perennial plants. Carefully managed, they could produce most of our animal foods with far fewer chemical inputs – sometimes with no inputs at all. That's why so many traditional societies have relied on them for a safe and dependable food supply.

When the first farmers began planting seeds back in Neolithic times, they chose the wild plants with the largest seeds. These were mostly annuals. From those plants they developed the first crop staples, emmer wheat (an early ancestor of modern wheat) together with wild barley. Today's high yielding varieties are the result of selective breeding from these early crop ancestors.

Even so, few societies in history have relied solely on annuals for their food supply. They found the harvests were too unreliable. While some communities were happy to rely solely on the foods of perennial plants – the foods of grasslands – many more maintained diets that included foods of both perennials and annuals. They found that life was more secure that way.

In Britain, as in other parts of Europe, our own version of this belt-and-braces policy was mixed farming in which grain crops for direct human consumption alternated with pasture which was grazed by livestock. After two or three years the pasture was ploughed up for a cereal crop. Though annual grains were important, the system benefited from the stability of perennials.

Today farmers around the world are ploughing up grasslands and sowing their fields with the new, high-yielding annual crops. In doing so they are making the world's food supply dangerously dependent on oil in the form of pesticides and chemical fertilizers. They are also reducing soil fertility – threatening the food supply of future generations – and exacerbating climate change by releasing greenhouse gasses into the atmosphere. Instead of helping to stabilise the global climate, modern high-yield agriculture is making things worse.

In a world increasingly worried about environmental damage and carbon footprints, the development makes little sense. In defence of modern food production, agribusiness leaders point out that crops such as cereal grains, oilseeds and the rest are easy to transport and store, less perishable than most animal foods and high in energy and protein.

But when you look at the damage they're doing to our planet and our future food security, it's an argument that's difficult to sustain. It begs the question – who benefits? Overwhelmingly it's large energy corporations, global food traders and the very biggest industrial farmers.

Somehow we've all been tricked into accepting at face value the PR case for the "green revolution" of the 1970s. The very phrase sounded environmentally benign, so we all bought into it. At the time we believed it to be the best way to feed a growing world population.

The singular achievement of the revolution was the battery of "miracle seeds" of the 1960s and 70s, the short-stemmed, high-yielding strains of wheat, rice and maize that the plant breeders developed, and which promised an end to hunger. But so far they've failed to deliver. What they have done is make food producers reliant on chemical inputs, effectively handing over control of our food supply to a handful of global corporations. When you look at the impact of this revolution on world climate and on the life-support systems of the planet, it's clear we can afford it no longer.

Not long ago I went along to one of Britain's top trade shows for arable farmers. It's called the Cereals Event and each year it's held in East Anglia, the country's main grain-growing area. I wanted to take a look at the arsenal of chemicals today's wheat growers spray on their crops between sowing and harvest.

For these big grain producers, the pesticide programme begins in autumn when the wheat plants are tiny. First they're sprayed with a mixture of two weed-killers plus an insecticide to destroy pests.

The following spring, while the plants are still quite small, they're sprayed with a chemical cocktail: two fungicides – pesticides designed to eliminate disease organisms – and a plant growth hormone to stop the crop growing too tall and falling flat in high winds. As the plants grow bigger they're given another chemical cocktail, this time containing three different disease-curbing fungicides plus a blend of growth hormones. During the most rapid stage of stem growth a third fungicide cocktail is sprayed on the crop. Finally, there's a spray just as the large "flag leaf" emerges at the top of the stem and the plant starts developing the "ear" with its tiny grains.

Along with all the chemical sprays, wheat crops are given regular doses of chemical fertilizer, particularly nitrogen. It's the lush, "watery" growth induced by fertilizers that makes modern crops so susceptible to disease. Hence the need for an endless sequence of pesticide sprays. Being annuals, the young wheat plants with their poorly-developed root systems can't survive without the chemical back-up.

Most British cereal growers produce wheat this way. Almost half the national crop is then fed to livestock. It would be hard to devise a more wasteful pattern of food production than this. To produce a kilogram of beef this way takes around eight kilograms of wheat grains; wheat that could be nourishing a lot more people if consumed directly.

Around the world the rush into cultivated crops continues unabated. Britain's dash for grains followed the country's entry into the Common Market in 1973. Thanks to the generous subsidies on offer from Brussels, UK farmers doubled their wheat area to five million acres, destroying large areas of grassland in the process.

Brazilian farmers are now embarking on a similar journey, though without the generous state subsidies. A number of large-scale operators are busy ploughing up savannah grassland to plant soybeans, a cheap source of proteins for intensively-farmed cattle.

One of the biggest companies in the game, Bom Futuro, operates 300 combine harvesters and 500 tractors in the production of more than 600,000 tonnes of soya a year.[2]

In many ways, the continuing flight from grass to arable crops is a re-enactment of the tragedy that took place more than a century ago on the greatest of all grasslands, the American prairies. As we've seen, today's intensive wheat growing was nurtured by 19th century settlers on the Great Plains. In the national mythology, these tough and resourceful pioneer families tamed the wilderness at America's heart, turning it into productive farmland. The facts tell a rather different story.

In reality this land, stretching west from the Mississippi to the foothills of the Rockies, was no wilderness at all, but a highly productive ecosystem supporting a wealth of life forms. A small patch of tallgrass prairie – the vegetation in the wetter eastern region - might easily contain as many as four hundred different plants, most of them non-grass species or forbs. These wild flowers and herbs occupied the spaces between grass plants, boosting soil fertility by bringing up nutrients from deep down in the soil and, in the case of legumes, by "fixing" nitrogen from the air.

A square metre section of tallgrass would have an underground network of roots and root hairs which, placed end to end, would stretch twenty miles. Two-thirds of the plant biomass of prairie grassland lay below ground. Down there the dense network of roots was constantly being renewed. As roots decayed and died, their functions were taken over by young replacements. Discarded roots were broken down and incorporated into the general stock of organic matter by the actions of soil micro-organisms, including free-living bacteria and thread-like fungi known as arbuscular mycorrhiza. Organic matter content of those fertile prairie soils was typically 10 per cent, though it could rise to 15 per cent or more. It was this rich storehouse of carbon compounds in living and non-living forms which sustained the unimaginable productivity of the prairie grasslands. Though the life of the prairies was made up of thousands of species, it was the vast herds of buffalo that showed the real productive power of grassland.

The American buffalo – *Bison bison* – weighed up to a tonne and stood nearly two metres high. At the peak of their population, their combined weight was greater than the entire human population of the United States and Canada today. And it was the prairie grassland that sustained them, along with fifty million pronghorn antelope, five million prairie dogs, elk, deer, plains grizzlies and wolves.

The prairies also nourished an army of unseen grazers. A single square metre of prairie soil contained over five million plant-eating nematodes; roundworms. These creatures munched their way through an even greater tonnage of vegetation than the bison herds, such was the power of the great grasslands to produce sugars from solar energy.

Without fertilizer or irrigation – in a climate where rainfall is low and droughts are frequent – the prairie grasslands supported a biomass far greater than our modern, intensively managed croplands. Sadly nineteenth-century America had other plans for them.

Not long after the arrival of Europeans, the Great Plains began to echo to the crack of the high-powered Sharps repeating rifle and the ring of the steel-bladed John Deere plough ripping through the root systems. Within a few years the grasslands and the buffalo had gone. In their place the settlers sowed wheat, the new Turkey Red variety which was tough enough to withstand the harsh prairie climate.

For a few years the settlers harvested bumper crops, nourished by a thousand years of fertility that had been built up under grass. An ocean of grain poured from the mid west granaries and was shipped around the world.

If the settlement of the prairie lands was to be successful, consumers "back east" had to be "educated" to buy this cheap new staple. In bourgeois 19th century drawing rooms the myth developed that high-protein foods were dangerously over-stimulating. The Reverend Sylvester Graham of Connecticut preached that sex was unhealthy because sexual emissions sapped the body's strength. A diet of grains would reduce the unhealthy expenditure of semen.[3]

By the 1890s, charlatans and social reformers were competing for the vast profits generated by patent cereal products. The resulting trade wars between the makers of competing brands of pap became known as "the corn flake crusades". The tussles still continue today as the manufacturers of over-processed, nutritionally worthless breakfast cereals advertise them aggressively as "healthy foods".

For the prairies the coming of annual crops spelled the end of the land's amazing productivity. In the dust bowls of the mid 1930s the degraded soils literally blew away. Soil experts blamed drought. But the prairies had always been subject to drought. Under their cover of perennial grasses and herbs they remained productive. But a few years under intensive wheat destroyed the organic matter, source of the soil's fertility and strength.

It came as a great shock to many Americans to see the billowing black clouds drifting across their cities; clouds not of smoke or water vapour but of soil particles. One particular dust cloud darkened the streets of Washington DC, just as Congress was about to debate the setting up of a soil conservation service.

Today, as we've seen, the prairie lands are still under annual crops, only possible because they are constantly dosed with chemical fertilizers and pesticides, and because the US government is prepared to spend billions of dollars a year on irrigation and public subsidies.

This tragic sequence has been repeated over and over again in Britain and around the world. Sustainable grasslands producing healthy foods are ploughed up in the great global lottery of cereal cropping. In the process fertility is lost and thousands of tonnes of carbon are released into the atmosphere.

Industrial arable farming is a major source of carbon emissions. Carbon is used directly through the use of fuel energy in day-to-day operations such as cultivations and harvest. On top of this there's the energy needed to produce its principal inputs, particularly chemical nitrogen fertilizer. Together nitrogen fertilizer, mechanical power and pumped irrigation account for 90 per cent of farming's energy inputs.

Because of its extravagant use of machinery, fuel and fertilizer, industrial agriculture uses far more energy than sustainable, low-input methods. In Britain, organic farms use less than half the energy per hectare of conventional farms.[4] In the USA, high-input industrialised farming systems such as maize or wheat growing consume up to 120 per cent more energy than low-input systems, even though the yields aren't that different.

This is why the ploughing up of grassland to grow cereal crops to feed to animals is, in energy terms, a singularly pointless thing to do, particularly as it produces poorer foods at the end of it.

There's one other critical source of carbon emissions, one whose dire consequences were graphically demonstrated following the ploughing up of the American prairies. It's the loss of soil organic matter that follows ploughing and cultivation; the everyday business of arable farming.

Soil organic matter is the term used for the total of all organic substances in the soil – decaying residues of dead plants, animals and insects plus the numberless mass of soil microbes and the substances they produce. This great reservoir of organic compounds is in a continuous state of flux, and it's what gives soils their innate fertility.

Organic matter helps to give soil its basic structure so it can retain air spaces that allow plant roots to grow. It holds moisture and plant nutrients so they aren't lost by being washed away to rivers and streams. Perhaps most important of all, it's the lifeblood of the soil's microbes, the vast population of bacteria, protozoa, fungi and the rest that enable plants to make healthy growth.

Soil organisms supply plants with nutrients, provide them with water and protect them against toxins and disease. Without the activity of soil organisms, life on this planet would quickly grind to a halt. Crop-growing with its routine ploughing and cultivation – plus its non-stop barrage of chemical fertilizers and sprays –

disrupts the living network and breaks down many of the organic compounds.

When land is ploughed and cultivated for a crop, organic matter is oxidised and carbon released to the atmosphere as carbon dioxide, thus adding to the total of greenhouse gases. When "virgin lands" like the American prairies are ploughed up, the level of soil organic matter starts to fall dramatically. After a number of years it often stabilises, but at a far lower level.

In Britain many soils that have been producing arable crops for years now contain very low levels of organic matter – often less than 1 per cent. In this condition the soil can't hold much water and is particularly vulnerable to drought. Nor can it do much to help plants take up essential minerals or trace elements. Chemical fertilizers may go on producing a harvest, but food crops from these over-worked soils are often depleted of trace elements. The good news is that, under grass, soils begin to rebuild their stocks of organic matter. This has profound implications, not only for the nutritional quality of the food we eat, but for the health of the planet.

Climate change is believed by many scientists to be caused by the accumulation of carbon dioxide in the atmosphere, mainly as a result of human activities. Over the past two centuries atmospheric carbon dioxide levels have gone up from 280 parts per million to 365 parts per million. Of the world's current emissions, 60 per cent is absorbed by the oceans, plants and other "carbon sinks". The other 40 per cent of human-induced carbon emissions stays in the atmosphere and helps speed climate change.

Much is made of the potential for carbon sinks to absorb more of the polluting gas. Reforestation is seen by many as the most promising way of "locking up" more carbon in vegetation. By contrast, the possibility of storing carbon safely in the soil hardly gets a mention. It suits those who profit from industrial farming to keep public attention away from farming and fixed on forests.

But the world's soils hold far more carbon as organic matter than all the vegetation on the planet, including forest. No less than 82 per cent of carbon in what scientists call the "terrestrial biosphere" – that part of the earth's land surface, plus the adjacent atmosphere, where life exists – is in the soil. Just as we have depleted soils of carbon by adopting industrial crop production, we could easily begin to put it back again by changing the way we grow foods. Even cereal growing could be made to capture carbon instead of releasing it.

Practices like reduced tillage and the use of cover crops help to increase the level of organic matter in the soil. In reduced tillage systems, seeds are planted in land that hasn't been ploughed, just lightly cultivated. Cover crops, such as rye or mustard, are grown between commercial crops to prevent the ground being left bare, providing root systems that will be broken down later by soil micro-organisms to produce organic matter.

These and other methods can be used to encourage carbon capture even under intensive crop farming. But producing food from grasslands offers far more exciting possibilities for reversing climate change. Organic farms which include grassland as part of their crop rotations can capture large amounts of carbon and put it back in the soil. In a long term experiment in Pennsylvania in the United States, organic systems, including clover, boosted the level of soil carbon from 1.8 per cent to 2.4 per cent.[5]

This is in line with British research results, showing that the level of soil organic matter under pasture land increased by more than 50 per cent in just ten years, while the organic matter content of adjacent cultivated land fell. These may not seem large amounts but they equate to almost a tonne of carbon captured each year across every hectare of farmland.

According to a Royal Society estimate, carbon capture by the world's farmlands could total as much as ten billion tonnes of carbon dioxide a year, given better management of the soil. That's more than the annual carbon dioxide accumulation in the atmosphere. A different form of agriculture – with more emphasis on grassland production – wouldn't merely help with the problem of global warming; it could solve it.

Carbon Farmers of America, a company selling "Carbon Sinks" to people who want to help reverse climate change, estimates that if the organic matter content of the world's farmed soils were increased by as little as 1.6 per cent, the problem of climate change would be solved. All the excess atmospheric carbon currently threatening our climate would vanish. Simply returning the American prairies to their pre-industrial fertility would, on its own, return global atmospheric carbon dioxide to pre-industrial levels.

In the southern hemisphere Australia is the first country to recognise the importance of soil as a carbon sink. In 2007 a group called Carbon For Life launched a soil carbon accreditation scheme. Through this scheme farmers are paid for every tonne of carbon they lock up in their soils. The group was founded by scientist Christine Jones who has campaigned for years to get politicians to understand the role of farming in countering climate change. Now at last she is making progress.

Her aim is to see Australian farmers building new topsoil by getting their soils to store more carbon than is lost to the atmosphere. Scientists used to believe it took thousands of years to create new soil through the natural weathering of rock. But by using pasture and the right grazing methods it's possible to put back carbon and quickly build new topsoil, even in deeply weathered and fragile soils like many in Australia.

Christine Jones thinks of soil as a renewable resource. In her view growing new soil is much like growing a tree. Both processes need carbon dioxide, water and light to fuel the production of photosynthetic materials. In trees, some of the carbon captured from the atmosphere combines with other elements to form wood.

In the soil, some of the carbon taken up by green plants combines with weathered mineral particles to form new topsoil. Grazing animals and microbes in the soil are essential to the process.

"Healthy grasslands can contain over one hundred times more carbon in the soil than on it. This makes a well managed perennial grass 'ley' the quickest and most effective way to restore degraded land."

It's also the most effective way to reduce carbon dioxide loading in the atmosphere. The process of building topsoil counters climate change, even as it provides the foundation for growing healthier foods. To put it another way, simply by buying grass-fed foods consumers alone could defeat climate change whatever the world's politicians decide.

Christine Jones's own estimate of what it would take to solve the world's greenhouse gas problems shows how straight forward it could be. She calculates that raising the level of soil organic matter by 1 per cent across just fifteen million hectares of land would capture the carbon equivalent of the earth's total greenhouse emissions.

According to the United Nations Food and Agriculture Organisation, the world's farmers currently devote around 1.4 billion hectares to growing grains. So if just 1 per cent were converted to pasture and grazed efficiently, greenhouse gas levels in the atmosphere would be stabilised. And the consumers of the foods they produced would be a good deal healthier.

Perhaps to deflect attention from this obvious solution to the climate crisis, big business agriculture makes much of what are claimed to be the environmentally-damaging effects of ruminant animals like cattle and sheep. The break-down of vegetation in the rumen – the animal's natural fermentation vessel – produces large amounts of the hydrocarbon gas methane. In its greenhouse effect, methane is 23 times more damaging than carbon dioxide.

Ruminants belch it out continuously, adding to global warming. The Food Climate Research Network estimates that meat and dairy consumption accounts for about 8 per cent of UK greenhouse gas emissions.[6]

But this is only half the story. Putting livestock back on species-rich grasslands would almost certainly reduce these emissions. Some traditional grassland plants such as the legume bird's-foot trefoil are known to reduce methane emissions.

In an EU-backed research project, scientists at the Rowett Institute in Aberdeen have been looking at a number of plants and plant extracts to see if they have benefits as feed additives.

The scientists have identified a compound called fumaric acid as a promising candidate. When added to the diets of lambs the chemical led to faster growth and reduced the animals' emissions of methane by 70 per cent. The institute is now working with a major chemical company to develop a commercial product that can be sold to farmers.[7]

However, the institute's press release didn't say much about the fact that fumaric acid occurs widely in many plants and herbs of field and hedgerow, among them angelica, common fumitory, shepherd's purse and bird's-foot trefoil. Can it be that methane emissions – which have led to the claim that ruminant animals are damaging to the planet – have only become a problem because we insist on feeding them on chemically-fertilized ryegrass monocultures?

There's strong new evidence to show that pasture-based livestock systems produce less methane – and have a far lower carbon footprint – than our current industrial farming methods.

Some of the most reliable figures come from a New Zealand agriculturalist now working as a consultant to British farmers. Under a programme called "Pasture To Profit", Tom Phillips is helping hundreds of dairy farmers cut their costs and boost their incomes by getting their production from grazed grass rather than bought-in feeds such as cereal grains.

Tom was incensed when he switched on a BBC Radio Four environmental programme and heard a leading grassland scientist claim that intensive, high-yielding dairy herds were more environmentally friendly than grass-based herds. One of the arguments was that, since all cows emitted similar amounts of methane gas however much milk they yield, it made sense to produce milk by industrial methods – keeping the animals in sheds and feeding them large amounts of grain. This way the methane emissions per litre of milk were minimised.

To Tom it's a simplistic argument that has led to precisely the wrong conclusions. Using comprehensive data from hundreds of pasture-fed herds, he has come to an entirely different conclusion. Not only does grazing result in lower methane emissions, its overall carbon footprint is far smaller than intensive, industrial systems. In his calculations he included the carbon dioxide equivalent of every input, - fertilizers and pesticides, the manufacture and use of machinery, concrete used in buildings and yards, animal medicines and straw bedding, even the energy cost of fences and trackways. When everything was included, methane emissions from pasture-fed herds were shown to be 20 per cent lower than in conventional, high-yielding herds. The overall carbon footprint per litre of milk produced was as much as 40 per cent lower on grassland farms compared with intensive farms.[8] When added to the potential of grazed pasture for capturing carbon in the soil, the environmental case for grass farming starts to look unassailable.

Soil scientists have long thought of humic acid as a key player in the storage of carbon in the soil. The term humic acid covers a group of complex carbon-containing molecules that make up humus, the soft, amorphous material in soil derived from decaying plant and animal remains.

But in 1996 a Maryland soil scientist called Sara F. Wright - working in an agricultural research laboratory in Beltsville – discovered glomalin. This tough, long-lasting compound is rapidly changing scientific thinking on the nature of soil fertility and the way carbon is held below ground. It seems this soil "super glue" may have a central role to play, not only in feeding the planet, but in halting climate change.

Glomalin is produced by arbuscular mycorrhiza, the thread-like fungi that form symbiotic relationships with the roots of most vascular plants – those containing special tissue for conducting water and nutrients. The compound is named after Glomales, the taxonomic order that this group of soil fungi belong to.

Arbuscular mycorrhiza form intimate contacts with their host plants. Their hair-like filaments, called hyphae, often penetrate the cells of the root system. The fungi take sugars from the plant, using the carbon to make glomalin. In return the fungal hyphae extend the reach of the plant roots, enabling them to penetrate spaces the roots alone would be unable to exploit.

The hyphae act as pipes supplying water and nutrients back to the plant. The fungi seem to use glomalin to seal the hyphae so they don't leak. The compound appears to be very durable. Tests have shown that it will survive intact in the soil for more than forty years. In fact its very toughness is the reason it has gone undetected by scientists for so long. To separate it from soil you have to immerse it in a citrate solution and subject it to intense heat for more than an hour.

Glomalin is a glycoprotein, a compound made from both protein and carbohydrate sub-units. Both sub-units contain carbon, which in total comprises 30 to 40 per cent of the entire molecule. Humic acid, once thought of as the main storage material for soil carbon, contains just 8 per cent of the element.

It's the physical characteristics of glomalin – and the fact that it can steadily accumulate in soils – that makes it so important to life on the planet. As plants grow, the fungal hyphae move down the root to establish new networks close to the growing tip. As hyphae higher up the root stop transporting nutrients, their protective glomalin is sloughed off.

Loose in the soil, the sticky material attaches itself to mineral particles of sand, silt and clay and to organic matter, forming clumps or "aggregates". These are what gives soils their "structure" – the physical characteristics that determine whether or not they can produce healthy crops. Glomalin creates a soil structure stable enough to resist wind and water erosion, and porous enough to let air, water and roots move through it. It's also able to hold water, protect beneficial microbes and resist surface crushing. In short it appears to be the key to soil fertility and life above ground.

The new discoveries go a long way to explaining why soil biology is at least as important as chemistry in growing healthy crops. Without a healthy population of arbuscular mycorrhiza in soils, most crops can't put on healthy growth. Because they're unlikely to access sufficient nutrients, they either fail completely or become sickly and stunted.

Many of the tools of modern arable farming – pesticides, chemical fertilizers and the plough – destroy these soil fungi. So perhaps it's no surprise that today's crops need so much protection from pests and diseases. It could also explain why arable land under continuous cropping for grains has lost so much soil carbon to the atmosphere and has had such damaging consequences for our weather systems.

Under grasslands, with their dense and undisturbed root systems, the fungi thrive. American scientists studying glomalin levels in cultivated soils found the introduction of "no-till" systems – planting seeds without first ploughing the land – led to a gradual build up of glomalin. But even after three years, the level was only a quarter of that found in the soil beneath an adjoining strip of grass.[9]

One of the remarkable features of arbuscular mycorrhiza is their ability to respond to rising carbon dioxide levels in the atmosphere by stepping up their production of glomalin. Scientists at the University of California used outdoor chambers to control the carbon dioxide levels on small areas of grassland in a three-year experiment. They found that when the gas reached a concentration of 670 parts per million in the atmosphere – the level it's predicted to rise to by the end of this century – the fungal hyphae grew three times as long and produced five times more glomalin than those at today's levels.

In effect there's a natural feedback mechanism in play – the higher the concentration of carbon in the atmosphere, the greater the rate of storage in soil, always assuming there's a healthy population of the fungi present to make the transfer. But we don't have to wait for carbon dioxide concentrations to reach critical levels. Scientists are convinced the rate of carbon capture can be increased by simply changing the way we manage our farmland, and particularly our grasslands.

The key to efficient carbon capture is good grazing. When a pasture is grazed each grass plant adjusts to the sudden reduction in the amount of leaf by reducing its root system. It's part of a re-balancing process that keeps the roots and aerial parts of the plant in equal proportions. When leaves are lost through grazing or mowing, roots die back to compensate, and glomalin is released in the soil. Then as the leaves grow back again, the plant develops new roots to restore the balance. In this way the amount of decaying root tissue and the level of glomalin steadily rise in the soil following successive cycles of grazing and recovery. The whole pattern offers a great opportunity, not only to step up the rate of carbon capture, but also to boost production of healthy meat and dairy produce.

Fifty years ago a visionary Australian called P. A. Yeomans came to similar conclusions and turned his arid, dusty corner of New South Wales into a lush and fertile oasis. Of course, he knew nothing about glomalin, but he recognised that by using the restorative power of grassland, it was possible to rapidly build fertile, productive top soil on land that was virtually desert.

Sadly his ideas were not widely researched or taken up at the time. Global agriculture was intent on going down the route of high-input cereal production. Had his techniques been adopted, the world might not now be facing the threat of climate change.

Percival Alfred Yeomans – he preferred to be known as PA – is well-known to enthusiasts of permaculture, the application of ecological principles to farming. In 1943 he bought his own farm, 400 hectares of mostly bare, weathered shale and sandstone near Richmond, New South Wales. He found that by using a special aerating machine to let oxygen into his grassland, (in the way gardeners spike their lawns), he could greatly increase the rate at which roots were broken down and organic matter was formed. Combining root aeration with irrigation and regular grazing, he was able to create 10cm of dark, fertile topsoil in just three years on land where there had been only loose red shale before. From his experience he developed his "Keyline Plan", a design service for creating beautiful and productive landscapes for both town and country.

PA's son Ken now runs the service.[10] He has no doubt that his father's ideas could both remove the threat of climate change and produce higher yields and better food for the world. He says: "Don't believe the lobby groups. We won't need to decrease our standard of living. We won't need to abandon the family car. Nor will we need to live the austere life of monks or ride to work on push-bikes.

"On the other hand, our food will taste better. It'll be more nutritious, we'll be healthier and, most certainly, we'll live longer."

4

How secure is your food supply?

It's a bright morning in early spring and I'm sitting in the middle of a pasture field in Shropshire. Just sitting seems the appropriate thing to do here. There's a distinct air of quiet "unhurriedness" about the place.

A little way off a dozen or so young beef cattle lie contentedly chewing the cud in the warm sunshine. The grass field we share still has the withered, dry stems of last year's seedheads. But amongst the remnants of dead and decaying leaves, the bright green blades of the new season's growth are pushing through.

All around, the blackthorn hedges are coming alive with a pale dusting of new leaf. From a nearby copse drifts the sound of songbirds. The world and its worries seem far away. It feels timeless and enduring; it is, in George Orwell's words, "the deep sleep of England".

On my drive here from Somerset the countryside had looked anything but sleepy. Everywhere in England it seemed, farmers were taking advantage of the sunny, windless weather to take tractors into their crops and give them another dose of chemical spray – a cocktail of disease-killing fungicides, perhaps, or a straw-stiffening growth hormone to stop the plants falling over.

Others were driving up and down the crop with fertilizer spreaders, dispensing chemical nitrate; another dose of stimulant to coerce the crop into producing just a little bit more grain at harvest time. Soon it will be followed by another shot of pesticide to reduce the risk of catastrophic loss from disease and pests.

Just getting the crop to this stage has already cost farmers a great deal of money. From now until the time it's been harvested, dried and safely stored in the grain silo it will remain at risk, hence the need for this ceaseless chemical coddling. They'll be up and down with the sprayers and spreaders as many as a dozen times over the growing season.

Then before the summer is over they'll be into the crop with combine harvesters that will have cost them as much as a sizeable family house. There will be a fleet of huge trailers and 150HP tractors to haul the grain to the silo. Over the following weeks massive lorries will negotiate Britain's rural roads, picking up the grain and hauling it off to the mills and food factories.

If it's wheat, some will end up in bread and breakfast cereals. But a good deal more will be milled and used in animal feeds. Some will be hauled to a deep-water port for shipping abroad. Elsewhere on the planet it will be turned into cakes or biscuits, or fed to animals housed in gloomy sheds. Some might even return to Britain as factory-farmed meat.

By the time it does, the farmer who grew the grain will have planted another crop and be up and down again with the pesticide sprayer. The soil will have lost a little more organic matter, and the earth's atmosphere will be carrying an even bigger load of carbon dioxide. Stripped of organic matter the soil will be more vulnerable to erosion by heavy rain and wind. And the new crop will be more susceptible than the last to disease or the effect of drought.

While all this feverish and expensive activity is taking place on arable farms across the country, nothing very much will happen on the little grass farm in Shropshire. Cattle and sheep will graze the grass. They'll stay out in the fields all year as is natural for ruminant animals. In the open air – and on pastures rich in clovers and deep-rooting herbs – they'll grow strong and healthy, immune to many of the ailments that afflict housed animals.

In due course they'll make the half-hour journey to the abattoir for slaughter. The meat will come back to the farm where it'll be cut up and sold in the farm shop. Customers will get the healthiest of meats with all the omega-3s and CLA that only a pasture-based system can provide. And the soils that grew the grass, instead of being impoverished, will be a little more fertile than before. The soil will be higher in organic matter with a larger army of soil fauna to recycle nutrients, store carbon and grow healthy plants. What's more that soil will go on delivering fine foods year after year, through drought and flood and storm. The soil fauna will be immune to spikes in the oil market and to soaring food demand from China. They'll produce an utterly dependable supply of good food for local people, just as they've done for a thousand years.

Yet politicians seem determined to wipe out this form of farming and rely instead on oil-dependent, globally-traded, pesticide-contaminated grains for our food supply. It doesn't make sense.

As it happens the small Shropshire farm where I'm enjoying the spring sunshine, at Tern Hill near Market Drayton, has once before been at the centre of a row over food security. Back in World War Two the government told the farmer he must plough up some of his old grassland to grow wheat for the war effort.

At that critical time in Britain's history the government, supposedly in the national interest, had taken on draconian powers to dictate the way land was farmed. Out in the fields and farmyards the policy was run by local committees who were a kind of agrarian enforcement squad, known as "War Ags". If they decided a farm was not producing as much food as they thought it should, they could have the farmer thrown off his land. Unfortunately their decisions weren't always very smart.

When they told farmer Arthur Hollins that he must plough up some of his heavier pastures and plant the land with wheat, he didn't have much choice but to comply. He knew only too well that on his farm cereal crops wouldn't feed as many hungry people as pasture. And so it turned out. Attempts to plough the often waterlogged ground quickly became a fiasco of mud and lost fertility. A measure aimed at improving the nation's food security ended up doing the very opposite.

After the war Hollins went on to prove his point about grass. He developed a farming system that needed no bought-in chemicals or animal feeds – one which produced large amounts of high-quality food, year in and year out. The whole system was based on the productive power of fertile, species-rich grassland.

Arthur Hollins had not benefited from a great education. He'd taken over the small Shropshire farm at the age of just fourteen following the untimely death of his father. By his own admission he made plenty of mistakes, particularly over the use of chemical fertilizers. But he was a keen observer of the natural world, plus he had a rare gift for thinking outside the box. Rather than rely on chemistry to control the nature, he reasoned that farming would be far more efficient if natural processes were allowed to work more-or-less unhindered. So he got rid of his plough. He decided it was causing too much damage and mayhem in the subterranean world of the soil. It was this seething "cauldron" of life below ground that created the right conditions for healthy plant growth. From now on these natural processes would be allowed free rein.

He also decided to leave his dairy cows outside on pasture all year round, reasoning that this was what would happen in nature. Each autumn he would close off some of the fields on higher ground, reserving them for grazing in January and February.

His unconventional methods were derided by many in the farming community. However, his methods produced extraordinary results. While spending nothing on fertilizer or feed, he was able to support a productive herd of over a hundred Jersey cows solely on the grass he grew on his small farm. What's more the animals remained in superb health. In the open air and on their natural, all-grass diet they suffered none of the ailments that afflict today's dairy cows. The average productive life of modern high-yielding cows is just three years. Many of the cows at Fordhall Farm continued giving high quality milk for fifteen years or more.

With his first wife May, Hollins turned the milk into a range of top-quality organic dairy foods, principally yogurt, a food scarcely known in Britain at the time. By the 1970s the little Shropshire farm was employing no fewer than fifty people making and marketing dairy products. They were sold in top stores around the country; some were even exported to Paris. So clear were the benefits of producing foods this way that Hollins and a handful of other grassland enthusiasts campaigned throughout the 1960s and 70s to get their methods more widely adopted. Here was a way farmers could make decent profits while supplying cheaper, healthier foods to the British people. But the farming establishment was far more interested in subsidies on offer from Brussels.

Under the EU's common agricultural policy farmers could make good money by ploughing up their grasslands and re-inventing themselves as specialist cereal growers. High input crop production was meant to free the world from hunger.

In the event it has made the world's food supply more precarious and increased the threat of hunger. For us in Britain it has made our food supply wholly dependent on imported oil – either as fuel to drive machinery or in the form of pesticides and fertilizers without which the system cannot work. What's more, by breaking down soil organic matter – and weakening microbial activity below ground – it has eroded our long-term ability to feed ourselves. It provides no security at all, and this at a time when the world faces the unprecedented challenge of climate change.

Arthur Hollins and his colleagues offered Britain a secure, low-cost food system. We turned it down in favour of a globally-traded commodity whose production is environmentally damaging and ultimately unsustainable.

During the 1980s, when thousands of farmers were ploughing up their pastures to join the EU-sponsored cereals jamboree, we were constantly told by farming leaders that the change was unavoidable. "It's the only way to feed a hungry world", they said. Yet even as they uttered the mantra, the European grain mountain was growing ever higher.

Together Europe and the United States maintained (at taxpayers' expense) vast grain surpluses which had to be sold off cheap to the Soviet Union, handed out in misdirected food aid or simply dumped on world markets below the cost of production. Far from ending hunger, the policy entrenched it by putting small farmers out of business, both in developing countries and in the industrialised world.

Today the same mantra is being voiced afresh. At the National Farmers' Union centenary meeting in 2008, president Peter Kendall, himself a commodity cereal grower, warned that the world faced the threat of food shortages. He spoke of Britain's "moral duty" to make its contribution to global supplies of food and bio-energy. At the same event Professor Robert Thompson from Illinois University forecast that an increasing world population, coupled with rising incomes in Asia, would lead to an "explosion" in demand for food. The world would need to double food production by 2050 if mass starvation was to be avoided. Dismissing organic food as an "irrelevance", he called for the widespread adoption of biotechnology to develop crops tolerant of drought, flood, disease and poor soils.

The warnings are simply the latest manifestation of a new campaign to boost high-input farming. Earlier Professor Bill

McKelvey, head of the Scottish Agricultural College, issued much the same prediction of looming food shortages. At a London press briefing he urged Britain to continue down the road of intensive farming. Organic farming would never feed the growing world population, he warned, - Europe would have to face up to using GM crops if food shortages were to be avoided.[1]

This is the view of Britain's farming "establishment", backed by the powerful corporations who supply the chemicals, oil and machines that keep the system going. Not surprisingly they seldom mention the one viable alternative to intensive arable cropping – pasture farming. But farmers around the world are discovering that the methods practised by Arthur Hollins in the 1970s deliver healthy foods cheaply and sustainably. And one of the best exponents is in the United States, birthplace of intensive grain growing.

Virginia farmer Joel Salatin likes wearing a wide-brimmed straw hat when working in the fields at Polyface Farm in the Shenandoah Valley. The favourite headgear of most American farmers is the baseball cap emblazoned with a brand name like Monsanto or John Deere. But as Salatin never buys GM seed or powerful tractors he's not happy about wearing either brand. Instead he invariably wears a hat made of straw – a product of grass, he says. To him this is appropriate since he likes to describe himself as a "grass farmer". What he does is harvest the sunlight, or rather his pastures do. Strictly speaking, of course, his straw hat is from a grain crop, a product of big arable, and dependent on fossil fuel. But you get his point.

Grasslands are essentially collectors of sunlight. A grass field acts as a large photovoltaic cell, intercepting incoming solar radiation and using some of it to power the production of sugars from carbon taken from the air as carbon dioxide. You could compare a grass leaf with a small solar panel. The difference is that in a pasture, leaves are set at different angles, which makes the whole canopy more efficient at gathering sunlight than a flat solar panel.

This is essentially how farmers like Joel Salatin make their profit. While intensive grain farmers base their production on oil – in the fertilizers, chemicals and diesel fuel they use as inputs - grass farmers make full use of energy from the sun. But to do this they have to become skilled at managing grazing livestock.

In the Shenandoah Valley Salatin raises beef, chickens, turkeys, rabbits and pigs on just a hundred acres of pasture, surrounded by and closely interconnected with forest. As each pasture field reaches the right stage of growth it's grazed, first by cattle and then by poultry, pigs and rabbits.

Underpinning the system is grass; not just a single species but a grass "community" made up from dozens of grass, clover and herb species. Across these diverse grasslands the animals are "pastured" in turn. First the beef cattle graze, then as they move on, the egg laying hens are introduced in their portable hen-houses. The hens peck grubs from the grass and cowpats, in the process spreading the dung and getting rid of parasites. The eggs they produce are tasty and rich in nutrients, while their own droppings fertilize the grass for the next batch of cattle to move in, once the grass has regrown.

This simple practice of rotational grazing, understood by

generations of farmers before the industrial era, produces large amounts of food. Each year the hundred acres of pasture at Polyface Farm produces about twenty tons of beef, fifteen tons of pork, ten thousand chickens, twelve hundred turkeys, a thousand rabbits, and more than four hundred thousand eggs.

These are extraordinary levels of production. Achieving them from intensive grain growing would damage both the soil and the people eating the less-than-wholesome foods. What's extraordinary about grassland farming is that it takes care of both.

For all their prodigious output, the pastures at Polyface Farm become more fertile and productive year by year. They require no pesticides or chemical fertilizers, and the food they deliver is filled with health promoting nutrients. They offer a secure food supply and a truly sustainable way to feed a growing population.

They also disprove the claim – repeated by supporters of modern, intensive farming – that GM crops will be needed to secure the world's food supply as weather patterns become more unpredictable. There's no doubt that climate change poses a severe challenge to our food supply. The extreme weather events we've started to see will impact on all ecosystems and have a big effect on crops, livestock, fisheries and forests.

In Britain the predictions are that we'll see more dry periods and, paradoxically, more incidents of intense rainfall leading to flash floods. Cereal cropping is extremely vulnerable to these conditions. Grassland systems, by contrast, are remarkably tolerant of them. Fertile pastures, with their higher levels of soil organic matter, will protect against both these threats.

Floods now take a heavy toll of both property and soil. Flooding incidents appear to be getting more frequent. The autumn of 2000 was the wettest for more than two hundred years. No fewer than ten thousand properties were damaged. In 2007 three thousand properties were affected by flooding, when more than double the average rainfall fell between May and July. According to the insurance companies, climate change could increase the annual cost of flooding in the UK from £1 billion to £25 billion.

Intensive arable production is one of the chief causes of flood damage. The steady destruction of organic matter – an inevitable result of continuous grain cropping – has reduced the soil's capacity to retain water. Instead of being held in the pore spaces of soil, heavy rain now runs straight off, frequently taking with it large amounts of topsoil. Soil erosion from cultivated land is now equivalent to an annual loss of a centimetre of soil across the whole UK land surface.

Fertile grasslands could protect both property and land. With their greater water-holding capacity they provide an effective "buffer" against sudden deluges, slowing the rate at which water reaches the rivers. Greater amounts of water are held in the soil, so the rivers don't get high enough to burst their banks.

In west Somerset, where I live, the roads and lanes often run red during sudden torrential storms. It can happen in summer or winter. It's the result of water cascading from the fields bringing with it tonnes of silt from the red soils. Cultivation for crops combined with an over-use of nitrate fertilizer has robbed the soil of organic matter, so there's nothing to slow the flow.

Before the rise of "big arable" and the nitrate fertilizers that support it, most of the sloping land round here was under species-rich grassland. It produced some of the finest beef in the world from Devon cattle, together with vitamin-rich butter and milk from cross-bred cows. And even after the heaviest deluge, the streams and rivers ran clear.

Attached to my own house on Exmoor we've got a small field so steep that the locals once called it "the Cliff". It has never been ploughed or had artificial fertilizers put on it. Each summer it's ablaze with wild flowers and herbs, among them salad burnet, rough hawkbit, meadow vetchling and bird's-foot trefoil. Our small flock of Exmoor Horn ewes seem to do well on it, and their lambs have grown at a tremendous rate. Despite its steepness and the thinness of the underlying soil, there's never been any run-off, no matter how severe the rains.

Were we serious about reducing the cost and heartache of flooding we'd surely surround our towns and cities with fertile grasslands. As well as giving us beautiful landscapes, they'd provide an effective solution to a growing threat. It would be hard to think of a better reason for protecting the controversial "green belts" around our towns and cities. The whole planning concept is under constant attack from developers who cite the desperate need for more housing. But under grassland these green areas could become a vital part of inland flood protection, at the same time providing a local source of pasture-fed fresh foods such as milk, cream, eggs and beef. They would also have the not inconsiderable advantage of protecting our food supply from the affects of drought.

The American prairies, with their incredible productivity, occupied the nation's arid heartland between the Mississippi and the Rockies. Even while they sustained the vast herds of bison, they were subject to regular periods of drought. The reason they stayed productive was because of their immense reserves of soil organic matter. Climate change may well produce more arid conditions on this side of the Atlantic. These are the very conditions that make cereal cropping look particularly hazardous. Without irrigation cereal crops are likely to fail in dry weather.

Irrigation has its drawbacks, too. It's expensive, costly in energy and wasteful of an increasingly scarce resource. In many parts of the world it is destroying topsoil through salination (contamination with salts). Salination is also caused by the replacement of deep-rooting perennial plants with shallow-rooting annual grain crops. Since the soil in these intensive systems can't hold as much water, saline groundwater is gradually drawn up nearer to the soil surface. After a while the land becomes too salty to grow crops and is lost to agriculture.

The Food and Agriculture Organisation of the United Nations says about one-tenth of the world's irrigated land has been damaged by salt, and about 1 per cent is lost to salt every year. According to the UN, this poses "a profound threat" to food security. In ancient Rome conquering armies used to spread salt on the land to starve their enemies. Through short-term chemical farming we seem determined to starve ourselves.[2]

In a climate increasingly susceptible to drought, pasture with deep-rooting herbs can provide a far more secure food supply. As the organic matter of their soils steadily increases, grasslands have the capacity to hold more and more moisture. At the same time deep-rooting herbs have the capacity to reach down to below-ground reserves during dry weather, maintaining a plentiful food supply for animals where cereal crops would fail.

At Polyface Farm, Joel Salatin manages his cattle by copying the grazing habits of the great bison herds. He believes they have much to teach us about creating fertile grasslands and building secure and sustainable systems of food production.

As they graze, bison herds stay bunched up in tight groups. This is mainly to deter predators, but for individuals in the herd it results in "aggressive grazing". The animal doesn't have a chance to be selective about the plants it eats. It must eat whatever vegetation comes its way as the tightly-packed herd moves relentlessly onward.

This natural pattern of grazing keeps the pasture highly productive. The vegetation is grazed quickly and evenly, then as the herd moves on, it has the chance to recover. There's a distinct "rest period" before the animals pass that way again. This allows the grasses and herbs to re-grow quickly, capturing more solar energy and locking up more carbon in the soil.

Salatin calls this intense but intermittent pattern of grazing the "pulsing" of pasture, much like a heartbeat. Using easily shifted electric fences he manages his own pastures this way. Bunches of cattle quickly graze small areas before moving on to the next paddock and allowing the grazed grass to recover. It's his prescription for producing large amounts of food without chemical fertilizers, machines or diesel fuel. He says: "Grazing can be done almost anywhere by anyone with any number of animals. It doesn't require combine harvesters, ploughs, tractors or buildings. It's also the fastest way to sequester carbon, collect solar energy and rebuild soil. Grazing is truly amazing."[3]

Half a century before American farmers like Joel Salatin began rediscovering the benefits of grass farming, farmers on this side of the Atlantic were starting to see it as the future for food production in Britain. With its maritime climate, this island off the north-west coast of the continent of Europe is ideally placed for growing lush grassland. Throughout the nation's history the finest foods have come from pastures – beef, butter, cheeses, geese, chicken, eggs, mutton, lamb and venison.

But to be productive pastures need skilful management. They are easily damaged or destroyed by both over-grazing and under-grazing. In the early years of the 20th century – when farmers were being hit hard by food imports – many pastures were neglected and allowed to revert to weedy scrublands. In Scotland one grassland farmer warned that this was precisely the wrong way to react to competition and falling prices. Among the hills of Roxburghshire he showed how pastures could provide Britain with a cheap and secure food supply.

Robert Elliot, a former tea planter in India, had taken up farming on the edge of the Cheviot Hills. There he had developed a farming system based on species-rich pastures, which, he discovered, could accumulate enough fertility in four years to grow several cereal crops without any chemical fertilizers. Nitrogen-fixing legumes like red clover and kidney vetch helped build up soil organic matter, while deep rooting herbs such as chicory and burnet made the pasture productive even during droughts.

He wrote that during the severe droughts of 1898 and 1899 his best field became "a veritable oasis surrounded by a girdle of scorched hills".[4] Grazed by the farm's Galloway cattle and cross-bred ewes, the pasture went on producing food while building up reserves of organic matter in the soil.

Elliot claimed that the natural wealth of the soil – exploited by grassland – would see farmers and the nation through hard times. It would provide cheap, nutritious feed for cattle and low-cost nutrients for growing healthy crops. There was no need for artificial fertilizers. A good pasture would keep farmers in profit even when the country was being swamped with cheap, imported food.

He might have added that the same good pasture would keep the nation fed if exporting countries switched to supplying China instead. It would keep the nation fed when the oil ran out or the price headed into the stratosphere. It would also keep the nation fed when climate change so altered weather patterns that droughts and floods became common events.

Elliot's ideas about food production attracted a good deal of interest in the early years of the 20th century. His book setting out the principles of grass farming ran to four editions and became a minor classic. But not until wartime food rationing did Britain's farmers seriously consider restoring their pastures. Even then it took the influence of a remarkable French scientist to get them started.

Andre Voisin taught biochemistry at the French National Veterinary School. He was a laureate member of France's Academy of Agriculture, and held an honorary doctorate from Bonn University. But at heart he remained a farmer, running a small farm near Dieppe that had been in the family for generations.

In the 1950s Voisin carried out a series of grazing studies to investigate the productivity of pastures. He developed a technique he called "rational grazing" in which cattle were moved around a succession of small paddocks rather than being allowed to graze over a whole field. He made the remarkable discovery that pastures grazed in this ordered way produced more food per hectare than arable crops.

It was an extraordinary finding. Had it been acted upon by the government and the farming establishment it might well have given Britain a healthy and sustainable food supply. The chances are there'd have been no BSE scare, and the fields and streams of this green and pleasant land would have been cleaner and less polluted.

Voisin's discovery was that, to be productive, pastures needed regular rest periods in the same way as manual workers in a factory. What made him think this way was a classic time-and-motion study carried out by Frederick Winslow Taylor for the Bethlehem Steel Company in 1890s America. The study involved a team of men whose job it was to carry ingots of high-carbon pig-iron. It was hard physical toil, and Taylor tried to measure the amount of work the staff could do before becoming fatigued.

To his surprise he found that the level of fatigue didn't depend on the weight of iron carried. The least tired workers were those who carried their ingots or "pigs" fastest. This was because they were able to take longer returning for the next pig without attracting the attention of the foreman. Taylor observed that when workers were given sufficient rest, they could shift three times more iron than before.

Voisin applied the same principle to the management of

grassland. No one had ever considered the needs of the plants before. By dividing up grass fields with fences, he was able to rotate the herd of grazing cattle around the various paddocks, giving the grass in each paddock a chance to recuperate before the cattle came back again. When pastures were allowed this rest period, they produced three times more vegetation over the season than when livestock were able to range over them at will.

When Voisin published his findings in a book called *Grass Productivity*, they caused much excitement in the world of farming. Here was an opportunity to boost food output without incurring great expense for the farmer. For a nation desperate to secure more home-grown food, the new findings held great promise.

British scientists took up the theme. William Davies, former director of the Grassland Research Station, urged the widespread adoption of mixed farming in which arable land was regularly sown with a grass crop to increase its fertility. He warned that land maintained under a monoculture of cereals often ended up in poor shape, particularly after a drought. There was also the risk of soil erosion when land was cropped with cereals for too long.

In phrases that seem even more relevant today, Davies wrote: "If the world is to feed itself better – and at the same time increase its population – it must farm its soils better than it has ever done in the past. It has become increasingly apparent that the grass crop plays a more fundamental role than any other."[5]

For a few years grass farming boomed. Hundreds of British farmers made the trip to Normandy to look at Andre Voisin's famous grazing pastures. By the 1960s the enthusiasm for grasslands and the foods they produced was at its height. But in the end grass lost out to cereal growing.

It was state subsidies that made the difference. So generous was government support for cereal growing, particularly under the EU's common agricultural policy, that farmers were prepared to invest in the necessary machinery and chemicals. Subsidies still drive this wasteful system. Even the new support for biofuels is, in reality, a grain subsidy in a new guise.

Ohio grass farmer Gene Logsdon believes modern, intensive grain growing is based on two myths. The first is that the annual tilling of the land for grain is necessary to keep the world fed. The second is that animals need to eat cultivated grains if they are to grow and produce "efficiently".

The modern farm animal market developed on the basis of these two misconceptions, says Logsdon. As a result we all now have to live under a corn and soyabean monopoly.

"Critics worry that pasture farming can't produce enough food to feed the world," he says. "In fact quite the opposite is true. There are millions of acres in the world that are amenable to grazing but are not cultivatable for annual grains. If we're going to see an ever-increasing population, pasture farming is an absolute necessity."[6]

Close to the village of Over on the Cambridgeshire fens, farmer Les Cook raises top-quality beef on species-rich grassland. Albany Farm is one of those rarities in eastern England, a small family farm. There isn't much more to it than a couple of hundred acres or so of rented land, some well-worn items of farm machinery and the bungalow where Les lives with his wife Anna and their three young daughters.

There's something else rather special about this place. It has a herd of pedigree Hereford cattle of the kind experts call "traditional". On a bright summer day Les drives me across the fields to see them.

In the lane leading to the grazing pastures he steers his Landrover between ruts and potholes. The rented fields border the River Ouse and are often flooded in winter. They form part of the natural flood plain. When the river runs high it often spills over the banks, just as it has done for thousands of years.

The low-lying grass acts as a natural sponge, temporarily holding excess water when the river is in spate. Some of the grasses in the pasture are coarse and stemmy, but the Herefords seem to thrive on it. As we park in the field gateway about thirty cows are lying contentedly with their calves.

The Hereford is one of the great pasture breeds of cattle that once made Britain stock-yard to the world. With the increase in cheap and plentiful cereals, they've mostly been supplanted by the bigger continental breeds that put on weight quickly on grain-based diets. But Les is convinced the Hereford is on the way back.

He explains: "In good pasture the Hereford will put on flesh quickly and efficiently. And on poorer grazing it will retain that flesh. The Hereford can thrive on next to nothing if it has to. Some of the big continental breeds may grow to an enormous size, but only when fed a lot of expensive grain.

"Then there's the taste. Nothing can compare with the taste of Hereford beef. It's well-marbled so it cooks wonderfully; a delicious, healthy meat. Hopefully people are starting to value these qualities again."

In the warm summer sunshine the cattle look magnificent with their rich, red coats and elegantly bowed horns. Standing quietly in the small grass field with its towering, unshorn hedges and distant view of Swavesey Church, they complete a picture that might have come from Constable.

Apart from sales of breeding stock, the beef from this farm goes to a butcher who specialises in selling high-quality meat. There's not much of a premium for it though it must be full of omega-3s, CLA and other health protecting nutrients.

Family grassland farms like this deliver a great deal more to the community than good food. They protect homes and crops from flooding, and they gather carbon from the atmosphere and lock it up safely in the soil. They also provide a safe, secure and local source of food, whatever happens to the world's climate and the international price of oil. That's why they should be counted among the country's greatest treasures.

5

The deserted countryside

In west Somerset there's a beautiful green valley with a long tradition for producing healthy food. Since many of the fields are steep and the soils are not particularly fertile, grass was traditionally grown as part of the crop rotation. The pastures, which invariably included clover, were essential for maintaining the productivity of the land. As a result, most of the foods produced from this part of the country were the foods of grassland – beef, lamb, milk, butter and cheese. These were the foods that kept small, family farms in business from generation to generation.

Not long ago one of the fields in the valley sprouted a collection of long, low sheds. It's as if someone had stuck a small trading estate in the middle of a pastoral landscape, which, in effect, they had. To me these sheds were instantly recognisable. This was an intensive broiler chicken enterprise. At the end of each building stood the characteristic feed bin for storing the imported, cereal-based ration that the birds would be fed. The farmer would buy in his chicks from a specialist breeding company, probably part of a global operation. He'd also buy in the feed, which might come from almost anywhere in the world. Then, when the birds were ready for the market, they'd be trucked off to a distant factory for processing. The meat would probably end up in a British supermarket or fast food restaurant. But it's not impossible that it would be shipped abroad. Every year tens of thousands of tons of this tasteless commodity are exported to be replaced by a similar quantity of equally tasteless imported product.

To describe chicken like this as "local" seems a nonsense. It's the product of a factory enterprise that could have been set up almost anywhere on the planet – France, Denmark, the USA or Thailand. Though this particular operation happens to have been located in Somerset, it's really part of the global economy. You couldn't even say this is a food that deserves to be called "British".

The product owes nothing to the local soils and very little to the local economy. It's stateless and anonymous, a food of the world. It's the poultry equivalent of a car assembly plant. The parts are made elsewhere and merely brought in to be bolted together. When the assembly-kit product is ready, it's shipped off to the great global market we're told is going to make all of us rich.

But when you look at the foods on offer in the local supermarkets it's hard not to conclude that we're really a good deal worse off for allowing the global market to invade our countryside. Compared with the foods these green, rain-washed hills used to produce, the stateless chicken looks a poor substitute.

This is not to blame the farmer who put up the new sheds. He has a living to make and a business to run. No doubt the economics came out fair and square on the side of the stateless chicken. And we British seem content to eat the stuff in enormous quantities.

Apparently in modern Britain roast chicken is the meal we most like to make at home. And when we eat out, the most popular meal choice happens to be chicken tikka. If asked I suppose most of us would say that chicken was healthier than red meat. That's what we've been led to believe by dietary experts. Yet the evidence is growing that many of the traditional foods that were once so demonised – beef, lamb, butter and whole milk – are, in fact, extremely healthy, especially when produced naturally from grass.

Can it be coincidence that the meat we appear to enjoy most just happens to be the one meat that uses vast amounts of cereal grains in its production? Cereal grains, one of the principal raw materials of the global food industry, make money for a whole lot of people: commodity dealers, shippers, chemical corporations, oil companies. Traditional foods from pasture make little money for anyone but the farmer. Maybe it's time we looked afresh at our so-called "preferred option".

In the days before oil-powered agriculture, small, local food producers were found all over Britain. Since there were no chemical fertilizers they depended on grassland to keep their soils fertile year after year. This sort of farming was particularly common in the west of Britain, where there had been no widespread adoption of the open-field system in the Middle Ages.

In west Somerset hundreds of small food producers survived until after the Second World War. In his book The Wisdom of the Fields, rural writer H. J. Massingham describes a wartime visit to the area. He stayed on a friend's farm in the "hillock and dingle country", the land between the Brendon and the Quantock Hills, close to the Bristol Channel. Here he met a number of small farmers, all producing copious amounts of nutrient-rich food from small areas of land. Grassland products featured strongly in their output.

The twenty-hectare farm where Massingham stayed produced beef from the local Devon breed and milk from crossbred cows. The farmer also raised pigs, sheep and poultry. All of them ran together with the cattle in the pasture fields, a practice known as mixed stocking. This not only increases the food output from every hectare, but also enriches the land.

The farmer, who already produced beef, milk, butter, lamb, bacon and chicken, was keen to add cheese to the list and to increase his production of butter, the author writes. This impressive output was achieved without chemical sprays and with almost no purchased fertilizer, the exception being a small amount of phosphate that went on the barley crop. With no other inputs, this small farm produced large amounts of the sort of foods that would today command a sizeable premium at farmers' markets.

Close to his friend's farm Massingham met a "Mr and Mrs Rowe", who also produced amazing amounts of food, this time on a tiny farm of less than two hectares, most of it steeply-sloping. As well as growing vegetables, potatoes and orchard fruits, the couple grew enough grass to support chickens, a small sheep flock and a breeding sow and her litter. "Enough food to feed a small hamlet," was how Massingham put it. If the whole country were farmed this way, he wrote, Britain would be able to feed a population of a hundred million people.

Not far away the writer met "Mr Meade and his wife". On just thirty hectares of hillside, this couple milked eleven cows and fattened sixty yearling lambs, as well as growing wheat, barley, oats, kale and root crops. Without using any chemical fertilizers, the Meades had doubled the output of their farm in just six years, at the same time increasing soil fertility.

Underpinning this production of healthy food was grassland and its power to harness the energy of the sun. In 1938, the year before the politicians took control of agriculture, there were almost a quarter of a million small farmers in Britain producing healthy food for local communities. Together they made up an army of independent entrepreneurs, working without state subsidies and producing foods by sustainable methods.

In the depression years between the two world wars, grassland, Britain's earliest form of wealth, saved the countryside. For many arable farmers a collapse in the world wheat price led to bankruptcy, but pasture-based livestock production thrived. Dairy farming boomed, and cattle, sheep and poultry farming all expanded.

In his classic book The Farming Ladder, George Henderson tells the inspiring story of one small farm's success in helping to feed the nation at a time of national austerity. George and his brother Frank took on a small, run-down Cotswold farm in the early 1920s, just at the start of the deepest recession of the 20th century. By traditional mixed farming based on pasture, the brothers turned their small, stony farm into a show-piece of productive agriculture.

They raised dairy cattle, sheep, pigs, geese and outdoor chicken, running many of them together on their fertile grassland. The more livestock they put on their grass fields, the more fertile the soil became. When the time came to plough up a pasture and sow it with wheat, it invariably produced bumper crops.

With the coming of war, government agricultural advisors brought parties of farmers to the Cotswold farm to show them how productive the land could be if managed properly. George himself wrote that if the whole of Britain were farmed in a similar way, the nation "would be self-supporting in food, except for citrus fruits and a few luxuries".

Tragically Britain betrayed these heroic food producers. The first attack came during the war – at the very time when they were doing their utmost to help the nation. The government committees who controlled farming made farmers plough up many of their most productive grasslands and sow the land with cereals. H. J. Massingham describes how Somerset farmers were forced to give up making butter and cheese as their forebears had done. They were told instead that they'd have to grow grains for the war effort.

While such executive actions might be justifiable when the nation's in peril, they didn't end with the coming of peace. The government began introducing the notorious farm subsidies which would heap rewards on large grain farmers and undermine the market for pasture-fed foods. Later the EU, with its grain mountains, completed the job by destroying the grass-based production that lay at the heart of Britain's sustainable, local food system.

As if this wasn't enough, the nation's independent food producers faced attack from a totally unexpected quarter. Health professionals began to brand the traditional foods of the countryside as hazardous to health. The advice was based on a theory known as the lipid hypothesis. The level of saturated fat and cholesterol in the diet was supposed to be a cause of coronary heart disease. It was an idea enthusiastically taken up by food manufacturers all too keen to denigrate traditional foods such as butter and milk, to promote their own factory-made vegetable oil spreads and soya dairy substitutes.

Today the saturated fat and heart disease theory has been blown apart. James Le Fanu, a doctor and writer, describes it as "the great cholesterol deception".[1] In not a single country does the amount of fat in the diet predict either the level of blood cholesterol or the risk of heart disease, he says. After half a century of research there's little evidence to show that low saturated fat diets prolong life.[2]

Despite the numerous findings, saturated fats and the animal foods they come from continue to be talked down by diet campaigners and the food manufacturing corporations who back them. Consumers are urged to limit their intake of red meat – even the healthy, grass-fed variety – and to choose low-fat milk. The foods that have sustained people for centuries are labelled "unhealthy", and the hard-working, independent families who produced them over generations are steadily pushed from the land.

In their place come the grain growers, large-scale producers of raw materials for manufacturing companies. Somehow we've all been led to believe that it's the factory foods that do us good: – the over-processed breakfast cereals and the starch-filled pastas; the clean, "pure" vegetable oils that are the source of deadly free radicals when heated; the soy products promoted as healthy foods though they contain an array of phytotoxins and hormone disrupters.

Carbohydrate-rich diets based on cereal grains are the root cause of obesity, diabetes and a host of other damaging conditions in western industrial societies. Yet the unhealthy foods that contain them are everywhere – in pasties and burger buns, in cakes and biscuits, in pizzas and pastries. We shun the healthy foods that keep family farms in business, yet we can't get enough of the calorie-rich fakes that empty the countryside.

Molly Dineen in her award-winning TV documentary The Lie of the Land gives voice to a group of mostly livestock farmers who feel themselves unvalued and unrewarded in our modern, consumer society. There's a particularly moving scene where a Gloucestershire farmer drives her around his village in the Landrover, pointing out all the smart country homes that were once small farms.

There's the little pig farm that has now become the valuable residence of a property developer; the mixed farm that has now become an all-arable unit. Even the village school has been transformed into a desirable country house. In the farmer's view a living community has been destroyed, and a way of life generations old obliterated.

As a beef producer he wasn't sure how long he'd be able to hang on himself. Society seemed unwilling to pay the price for this sort of traditional food production. In the view of farmers interviewed in the film the blame lay principally with the big supermarkets. Their ruthless buying policies were forcing farmers to choose between running factory-scale operations and getting out, or so it was claimed.

The real causes are rather more complex. This isn't to deny the power of the supermarkets. Without doubt their treatment of suppliers can be tough and uncompromising. However, the decline of the rural economy and the breakdown of rural communities predates supermarket dominance. It has more to do with the rise of intensive cereal growing and the supremacy of "big arable".

For centuries it has been the culture of grasslands, and the animals they support, which has kept people living and working in the countryside. Whether on the permanent pastures of the western uplands or the grass leys of the lowland mixed farm, the care of livestock kept skilled people living on the land.

Crop growing, by contrast, is highly mechanised and requires far fewer people. Big, gas-guzzling machines have replaced most of the traditional, skilled workers. Pesticides and weed-killers – which substitute chemicals for labour - got rid of many more. When the growing mountains of surplus grain began to be fed to livestock on a large scale, the writing was on the wall for family farms and the rural communities they gave life to.

When laying hens are packed into battery houses and fattening birds are crowded into broiler sheds, the principal aim is to reduce labour costs – to get rid of skilled staff. As a student in the 1960s I well remember a novel method of rearing pigs, charmingly known as the "sweatbox" system. The idea was to crowd the animals into a small humid space so they'd have no inclination to do anything but lie around on their concrete floors. If they weren't allowed to burn up energy by moving about, so the theory went, they'd convert their feed into meat more efficiently. Methods like this made the traditional, outdoor-rearing of poultry and pigs uneconomic. In doing so they spelled the death-knell for the small family farm.

An elderly woman, who had grown up on a Somerset farm,

once showed me the ancient cash book her mother had kept during the recession years of the 1930s. Everything sold by or bought for the farm was entered in this little book. What surprised me was the contribution that sales of eggs made to the overall viability of the farm. Each week a few dozen eggs sold around the village brought in a useful income and helped keep the farming family in business. In those pre-war days thousands of West Country farms ran small poultry enterprises, mostly running the birds outside on pasture and selling either eggs or chicken to the local community.

With the growing surplus of cheap, subsidised grain in the 1960s a different sort of poultry industry began to emerge – the intensive, indoor model. Often backed with "city" money, the new big-business investors built large-scale broiler and battery-cage operations, making use of the cheap grains. In a few short years they virtually took over poultry and egg production in Britain, and what had been a valuable enterprise on the family mixed farm was gone.

Pig production followed a similar pattern. Until the mid 20th century, the keeping of a few pigs was an option open to pretty much every family farm in Britain but cheap cereals put an end to it. The big investors moved in and put up their large-scale factory operations, throwing thousands of skilled herds-people out of work and further undermining the viability of the family mixed farm.

Not even ruminant animals were safe from the inexorable advance of big arable. During the 1980s, when EU subsidies made it profitable for dairy farmers to squeeze ever more milk from their long-suffering cows, many took to feeding large quantities of cereals. They even bred a special cow for the job – the high-yielding Holstein.

In this way big business and its weapon of choice – industrial wheat – ruined the family mixed farm by picking off its enterprises one by one.

It's the advance of grain, with its dependence on cheap oil, that has done most to break up rural communities and empty the countryside of working people. The landscape of arable cropping is one of large machines and holiday homes. The pastoral landscape – the landscape of grass and livestock – is one of thriving village communities and diverse wildlife populations. It's also one of work and commerce.

For lobby groups like the Countryside Alliance and the National Farmers' Union, it's easy to attack the government for closing rural post offices and village schools. What they're less willing to acknowledge is the part played by farm policies – and by implication some farmers – in the erosion of village communities. The rise of grain and its take-over of livestock production have played a big part in the loss of rural schools, post offices and pubs.

It's a story that's as old as Britain's history. The Biblical struggle between cultivators and grazers, the story of Cain and Abel, has been re-enacted on this island for centuries. Back in feudal times, cultivation and wheat growing was the business of the lord-of-the-manor. Being a cultivator meant being wealthy enough to afford ox teams, a capital investment well beyond the reach of most peasant farmers. But even the poorest members of the community could survive and prosper by running their own cattle or sheep on their small rented holdings or on the communal grassland.

In the early 13th century, a group of "unfree" tenants on the great Glastonbury Abbey estate owned between them a bigger sheep flock than their landlord, the abbot.[3] In Shakespeare's England, the rural landscape was divided between "champion" country – mixed farming areas where arable cropping took place alongside grassland and livestock husbandry – and what was known as wood pasture. In these partially wooded areas most farmland was down to pasture, and dairy farming and cattle rearing were the main enterprises.

The communities of wood pasture areas comprised a core of indigenous peasants with their own holdings, together with a growing number of poor squatters and travellers. In the "champion" country, wealthy bankers and merchants were enclosing large tracts of countryside, dispossessing poor people of their traditional grazing land. But the pastoral way of life of the wood pasture provided security at a time of widespread social upheaval.

Grassland continued to protect rural life well into the 20th century. When the wheat price collapsed early in the century, and again after World War One, Britain's rural community looked to pasture to carry them through. A fast expanding dairy industry, and thriving markets for pasture-raised poultry, eggs and beef, kept country people working through the dire recession years between the wars.

A revival of pasture-based farming today would bring new life to the countryside. Linked to an expansion of local food markets, it would brings jobs and wealth back to village Britain. In a competitive, technological world the provision of rural jobs might not, on its own, justify an expansion of grassland farming. But when added to the benefits in food quality and carbon capture by the soil, the case starts to look unassailable.

A return to pasture farming would mark no triumph of romanticism over realism. On the contrary, it would denote the return of rational food production in an age when climate change, rising commodity prices and the volatility of global markets make our present food production methods look decidedly shaky.

When grassland scientist Sir George Stapledon urged farmers to put grass leys at the heart of their rotations, he was campaigning as much for prosperous family farms as for efficient food production. Though not committed to organic agriculture, he strongly opposed the rise of monoculture and the large-scale specialist farm. He believed the abandonment of mixed farming and grass leys would lead to disaster.[4]

Today food production by monoculture has become the global standard. It is practised everywhere with a handful of annual crops on which the world's food now depends. Around the world productive and sustainable systems are in retreat. And as they go, thousands of small farmers are thrown off the land. Where Britain's rural dispossessed once took refuge in wood-pasture areas, urban shanty towns have become the enforced destination of many small farmers in poor countries today.

Food campaigner Vandana Shiva describes industrial grain production as "war against farmers and the land". In her own country of India she saw the seeds of the Green Revolution – which won the Nobel Peace Prize for its inventor Norman Borlaug – produce mass bankruptcies and suicides among the farming population it was supposed to help. Far from increasing their profitability, the costly seeds, fertilizers and pesticides that went along with it plunged farmers into a spiral of debt.

At the same time it so depleted soil organic matter that, while grain yields increased, the overall biomass supported by the land went down. This resulted in a "fodder famine", leaving farmers unable to feed their livestock. Worse, it meant the soil was unable to hold as much moisture. The search for high yields of grain increased the risk of drought and desertification.

Shiva trained as a quantum physicist and expected to spend her working life grappling with the questions of quantum theory. Instead she has spent more than twenty years puzzling about the contradictions inherent in industrial agriculture, particularly intensive grain production.

Why, she wondered, were Indian peasants being pushed into debt and penury by a system of agriculture that was supposed to bring prosperity to rural communities? And why did monocultures, which were intrinsically of low productivity, come to be accepted as highly productive though they required huge inputs of chemicals and fossil fuels, and then produced less food than traditional, diverse farming systems?

Shiva, the physicist, has begun to find answers to her questions. Though they are answers that apply specifically to her native India, they are equally relevant to Britain, Europe and America. In fact wherever nations have allowed industrial agriculture to displace traditional, biodiverse farming, the answers carry an awful warning.

Traditional farming systems are based on rotations that can include cereals, legumes and oilseeds. In Britain those systems also include a variety of food animals to harvest the crops. It's not that grains weren't of interest to traditional farmers. On the contrary, they were regarded as a food rather than a commodity. While good yields followed the ploughing up of a fertility-building grass "ley", quality was of supreme importance. On mixed farms, the high level of organic matter and teeming biology of the soil filled grain with health-giving nutrients.

Modern grain monocultures are concerned with quantity; with yield; with the number of 150HP tractors needed to haul the grain from every wide, open factory-field. They're made to look productive because output is measured only as grain yield per hectare compared with the grain yield of traditional mixed farms. But if the whole food output of the mixed farm is included – the meat and milk as well as the grains – the mixed farm is invariably more productive.

Monocultures don't occur in nature. They're too unstable. Natural ecosystems are always diverse – they contain a wide mix of species. This is what makes them stable and productive, whatever the climatic conditions from year to year. Traditional farmers copy nature by building diversity into their own farming systems. It provides communities with more food and greater security. It's why, in an increasingly uncertain world, Britain needs more farms like this, not less.

There are plenty of examples in western agriculture to prove Shiva's claims. When George Henderson took on a small, worn out farm in the 1920s and decided to practice traditional mixed farming, he proved that given enough farms like this, Britain could easily be self-supporting in food.

Henderson had no doubt that small farms would always out-yield large specialist farms, so long as output was measured as food production per hectare. He compared the output of his own small mixed farm of thirty-four hectares with that of what he called large, well-managed farms.

He quoted wartime figures published in the Daily Telegraph for three well-known estates, ranging in size from four thousand hectares to twelve thousand hectares. Their outputs were one-third or less than those achieved by Henderson and his brother on their small Oxfordshire farm.[5]

As an agricultural student in the 1960s I saw dozens of examples of highly-productive family farms. In north Wales, where I lived, the output of many small upland farms was extraordinary, mainly because of their skilled management of grazing pastures. As prodigious food producers they outstripped by miles the production of specialist grain farms.

What made them seem uncompetitive was their high labour costs. This mattered not one jot to those farming families. They accepted hard work as part of the job. But large grain farmers were able to make themselves look efficient by replacing staff with big tractors and machines. While this put the right numbers on the balance sheet, it greatly reduced Britain's ability to feed itself should the need arise again.

Guardian columnist and environmental campaigner, George Monbiot, has no doubts about the superiority of small farms as food producers.[6] In terms of food produced per hectare of land, there's an inverse relationship between the size of farms and the amount of crops produced. The smaller they are, the greater the yield. According to Monbiot, the differences can be enormous. In a study of farming in Turkey, for example, farms of less than a hectare were found to be twenty times more productive than farms of more than ten hectares. Similar observations have been made in many countries, including India, Pakistan, Malaysia, Java, the Philippines and Brazil.

"If governments are serious about feeding the world, they should be breaking up large landholdings, redistributing them to the poor, and concentrating research and funding on supporting small farms," says Monbiot. However, this is not likely to happen in a hurry. Instead rich countries use subsidies to help their own large farmers compete unfairly with small farmers in the developing world.

At the same time, big business kills small farming by extending intellectual property rights over basic agricultural resources, including seeds. By developing crop plants that either won't breed true or don't reproduce at all, big business ensures that only those with access to capital can cultivate the land.

"The prejudice against small farmers is unchallengeable," adds Monbiot. "It gives rise to the oddest insult in the English language: when you call someone a peasant you are accusing them of being self-reliant and productive."

The justification for intensive grain production is that it's the only way to feed a fast-rising global population. It's a piece of modern mythology dreamed up in the boardrooms of chemical companies and energy corporations. They portray any suggestion that small farmers using traditional methods can feed the world as naive or deluded.

Yet the facts are clear to those who care to look. Sustainable, diversified agriculture as practised by small-farms is more productive per hectare than chemical-dependent, industrial grain production. And while traditional, small-scale agriculture leaves the land in good shape to feed future generations, industrial grain production robs the land of fertility and destroys the rural communities that could truly feed the world.

For Vandana Shiva this adds up to an over-whelming case for protecting country people and traditional farming. She says: "It's clear that industrial [plant] breeding has actually reduced food security by destroying small farms and the small farmers' capacity to produce diverse outputs of nutritious crops. Protecting small farms that conserve biodiversity is a food security imperative."[7]

It's sometimes hard to accept that the older, traditional way of doing things was best. We're accustomed to the idea of progress – that things improve and that the new is invariably better than the old. I remember an organic farming friend of mine once putting up a big sign in a field of wheat, grown as part of a rotation after three years in pasture. The crop looked amazingly good, so my friend put up a sign saying: "This wheat was grown without chemical fertilizers or pesticides".

A few days later an irate fertilizer salesman appeared in his yard. He'd been driving by on his way to an appointment when he'd seen the sign. He'd been so incensed he had called in to complain. The crop looked so healthy it must have been dosed with chemical fertilizer and sprays, he insisted. The message on the board was clearly a lie.

This a view held by most of Britain's farmers – especially the bigger ones. It's also shared by politicians, farming leaders and, sadly, some scientists. It's what Shiva describes as "the monoculture of the mind that blocks the creation of abundance on our small farms".

Yet whether it suits our world view or not, it's the small family farmers and their traditional pastures that will feed us, our children and our grand-children if we'll let them. And since no government seems prepared to do anything to ensure their survival, we'd better be sure of doing it ourselves.

6

A brief digression on the nature of grasses and grazing

Grasses – known scientifically as the Poaceae – evolved almost seventy million years before the first human beings walked the earth. Yet the fortunes of the two families are inextricably linked. The Poaceae, with ten thousand species, and the Hominidae, with just one member species, have become tribes of mutual dependence.

In the plant world, the grasses are colonisers, the early occupiers of disturbed ground. Human beings are the supreme creators of disturbance. They bulldoze the forests, and plough and cultivate the soil. In doing so they make opportunities for grass. In return the grasses supply our food, provide playing spaces, green our cities and refresh our air. The two families were made for each other.

Grasses are well adapted to exploit the environmental changes set in train by Homo sapiens. From among the angiosperms, the flowering plants, evolution has equipped grasses to be both versatile and highly mobile. Unlike other plants they have abandoned the habit of laying down woody tissue as a way of gaining strength. Instead they have opted to move quickly into the reproductive phase of their life cycle, speeding the rate at which they can colonise new ground. They have chanced their survival not on strength and durability, but on their speed of occupation. It's an adaptation that has made them the most successful plant group on the planet.

In its early growth stages the grass plant consists of a collection of shoots or "tillers", each made up of leaves growing from the base. No stem is visible. The true stem, at this stage highly compressed, lies hidden beneath the layers of tightly rolled or folded leaves. Active growing points – at the tip of the stem and at the bases of the leaves – are close to the ground surface and well protected from grinding molars and the whirling blades of mowers.

The leaves themselves can be crushed, hacked off or burned brown in the blazing sun. But from countless little engines of growth buried deep beneath the remnants of foliage, the first shoots of a new turf are already being formed. With the passing of the grazing herd or with the coming of rain, the grassland community is able to renew itself by growing replacement leaves and new roots.

With their protected growing points, grasses are able to thrive in the most extreme conditions. Only two flowering plants have been found to survive in the Antarctic circle. One of them is a grass, Antarctic hair-grass.[1] The Victorian botanist and director of Kew Gardens, Sir Joseph Hooker, was amazed to discover sheep's fescue, a stalwart of low-lying English meadows, growing at a height of almost 5,500 metres in the Himalayas.[2]

On America's Great Plains, species of grama grass flourish both on the prairie grasslands and at heights of over 2,000 metres in Arizona, enduring temperature extremes ranging from 38 degrees to minus 40 degrees centigrade.[3] But the award for survival acts must surely go to Lalong grass, which has been found growing in the mouth of a volcano in Java.[4] There it thrives in the swirling, sulphurous fumes; an innocent at the entrance of Hades.

In temperate conditions grasses need grazing animals to survive. In cool, damp climates such as Britain's, grassland is not the "climax" vegetation. Without regular grazing shrubby species will begin to take over. Given long enough the land will return to forest. For grasslands to survive, the animals must return from time-to-time and graze down the woody species before they become established. This is why human beings – with their domesticated livestock – are good friends of grasses.

When humans first appeared, the great natural grasslands of savannah and prairie already supported vast populations of mammals. But to extend their territories the grasses needed to begin colonising the forest areas. Enter the Homo sapiens right on cue. Soon the aggressive hominids started clearing the forests and creating open tracts of pastureland for grazing their cattle and sheep. The grasses had embarked upon a great process of colonization.

In the language of history, human beings are said to have domesticated the grasses. But in the language of ecology, the grasses may as easily be said to have domesticated the hairless apes.

Today the pasture field is the arena in which grasses and humans enact their ritual encounters so both can thrive. In the process of photosynthesis the leaves of pasture plants capture sunlight, using the energy to convert carbon dioxide and water into simple sugars. More than 90 per cent of a plant's dry weight is made up of organic compounds derived from these simple sugars.

Green leaves, like all living tissues, also respire; they burn sugars to produce the energy they need for metabolism, releasing carbon dioxide and water in the process. In effect it's photosynthesis in reverse. In bright sunlight the carbon converted into sugars is far higher than the carbon lost in respiration. So the pasture becomes more dense. But at low light levels the rate of photosynthesis falls. As the growing grass gets thicker, more leaves are shaded by those above them. Eventually a point is reached when more sugars are being burned by respiration than are being formed by photosynthesis. When this happens the older leaves start to die back and much of the production is wasted.

The farmer's job is to move animals onto a pasture, or a part of the pasture, while it's still growing and adding vegetation. The trick is to move them to the next pasture area before they've grazed too close to the ground. If the animals graze too much, there won't be enough leaf tissue left for the grass to recover quickly. The plants will have to draw upon carbohydrate reserves in the roots; a process that can delay recovery by several days.

At the start of the growing season or following a spell of grazing, pastures follow an S-shaped sigmoid pattern of growth. Early on there's a period of slow but accelerating growth. Then there's a period of rapid growth, followed by a spell of slow and declining growth. Knowing how to manage this recurring pattern of growth and re-growth is the art of good grazing.

It's an art known to generations of farmers and graziers before the era of cheap oil provided an easier, industrial alternative. In Thomas Hardy's time dairy cows were frequently moved on to fresh pastures. It was the established way to keep up production. Shepherds used their dogs to confine sheep to a small area of grass before moving them on to the next.

Edinburgh-born James Anderson, inventor of what became known as "the Scottish plough", is best remembered for his theory of ground rent, an idea taken up by the English economist Ricardo. But in a text dated 1791 he also gives a full and lucid account of what's now known as rotational grazing – the practise of grazing a small area of pasture in a paddock, then moving the animals on quickly to the next paddock.

Anderson wrote: "As every kind of animal delights most to feed upon fresh plants that have newly sprung up from a bare surface, in which there is no decayed or rotted stalks of any kind; there can be little doubt but that, if cattle that are intended to be fatted were always supplied with a constant succession of this kind of food, they would be brought forward in flesh as quickly as the nature of that food could in any case do it." He then suggests dividing the pasture field into fifteen or twenty equal "divisions".

He continues: "Instead of allowing his beasts to roam indiscriminately through the whole area at once, he collects the whole number of beasts that he intends to feed into one flock, and turns them all at once into one of these divisions; which, being quite fresh, and of sufficient length for a full bite, would please their palate so much as to induce them to eat it greedily, and fill their bellies before they thought of roaming about, and thus destroying it with their feet.

"If the number of beasts were so great as to consume the best part of the grass of one of these enclosures in one day, they might be allowed to remain there no longer; giving them a fresh park every morning, so as that the same delicious repast might be again repeated.

"And if there were just so many parks as there required days to make the grass of these fields advance to a proper length after being eaten bare down, the first field would be ready to receive them by the time they had gone over all the others; so that they might thus be carried round in a constant rotation."[5]

Anderson's description more than two centuries ago is a pretty fair summary of the modern system that is leading to a revival of pastoral cultures in the United States, Australia, Britain, France and a number of other countries. Modern practitioners might contest the idea of having the grass "eaten bare down". They'd argue that there has to be enough leaf tissue left at the end for the grass plants to go on photosynthesising, allowing the pasture to recover quickly. But little else has changed over two centuries.

Given that the system leads to such a big increase in productivity, it seems odd that it hasn't been more widely adopted. Can it be the farming world had to await the invention of the electric fence as an easy way of splitting up pasture fields into small paddocks?

According to Andre Voisin, the French biochemist and farmer whose studies on rotational grazing led to the current revival, there's a bit more to it than this. It seems that some of the early pioneers of the system failed to take account of the pasture's need for rest between grazings. As a consequence they didn't get the higher productivity that Anderson had promised, so they lost interest in the technique.

Today's generation of graziers are more considerate of the needs of grass plants. They've realised you can't just have a set number of paddocks and return the animals at fixed intervals through the season. You have to take account of growing conditions. For example, grass takes longer to recover from grazing in the late summer than it does in early summer when growth is going flat out. Likewise, in spells of dry weather pastures can't grow at the rate they'd achieve given plenty of moisture. There has to be some "slack" in the system to allow for these natural variations.

As Voisin put it in his classic book, Grass Productivity, which underpins the new grazing revolution: "Grass, like workers, needs rest. In the course of a grazing season, grass needs rest to renew its strength, just as the worker... has to rest to relax his muscles. Given this condition it will treble its productivity."[6]

Successful grazing also has to take account of the animals' needs. In Britain the principal grazing animals are cattle and sheep, both ruminants. They don't directly digest the vegetation that makes up the bulk of their diets. Instead the food is passed into the rumen, a large fermentation chamber where the material is broken down by the action of microbes. Most of the soluble nutrients are released this way, though unfermented fibre - together with some other materials – passes through to the lower gastrointestinal tract for digestion by enzymes.

As so much of the ruminant diet is made up of cellulose, it

seems odd that ruminant animals haven't evolved enzymes capable of breaking it down, relying instead on microbes in the rumen. Cellulose is a polysaccharide, a compound constructed mainly of glucose units linked together by a special chemical bond. Cellulase, the enzyme capable of breaking this bond, is produced by a number of bacteria, fungi and seedlings, but not by animals.

Cellulose is the main structural polysaccharide found in plant cell walls. It's one of the most abundant of all compounds found in living organisms. So it's something of a conundrum that animals existing mainly on vegetation don't have the means of digesting it directly. Vermont agronomist and grazier Bill Murphy thinks the life-style of grazing animals may have been the reason for the development of the rumen.

With few defences against predators, grazers would probably have left the protection of the forest for as little time as possible. They'd have quickly eaten their fill of plants growing in exposed clearings of the forest or at the forest edge, then retired to the safety of the trees to digest the food.

Instead of producing cellulose to digest the food immediately, they came to rely on vast numbers of symbiotic micro-organisms living in the digestive tract. These break down fibrous and soluble plant material by fermentation, effectively becoming the animal's cellulase-producing tissue. It's a slow process, but one well suited to an animal that spends a minimal amount of time gathering food and long periods lying quietly in hidden places.[7]

Ruminants use grass by first swallowing it, then later regurgitating the coarser material as cud. In a safe place the animal chews it a second time before swallowing it back into the rumen.

There volatile organic acids such as acetic, propionic and butyric acids, produced by rumen micro-organisms, become the animal's main energy sources. Micro-organisms also supply amino acids, the essential building blocks for proteins, together with vitamin K and B vitamins.

Virginia grass farmer Joel Salatin is convinced that for any grazing system to be successful it must take account of the natural behaviour of grazing animals. The world's great grasslands have been maintained and stimulated over aeons by herds that act in particular ways.[8]

First they stay bunched up in a tight group to deter predators. This close grouping means the animal can't be "picky" about the particular plants it eats. It has to eat whatever's in reach even if it's only a bunch of thistles. It can't be too careful about where it places its hoofs, either. This means that the turf gets well churned up, a process that stimulates biological activity.

Then there's the fact that wild herds move. They never stay in the same area for long. They are constantly moving onward like some restless, foraging tribe. This day-to-day migration spreads excrement over the whole landscape, says Salatin, while keeping the animals ahead of their parasites and other pathogens. It also provides the pasture with its essential rest period between grazings. Rest periods mean the grass grows better and more carbon is captured in biomass, the total mass of living material.

Thirdly, there's the key fact that native herds don't eat grain or fermented forages. Nor, it should be added, do they eat distillery waste, fruit syrups, biscuit crumbs, bakery waste or citrus fruit pulp, all materials that are regularly fed to ruminants in Britain.

Salatin says: "The beauty of the herbivore is, clearly, its ability to turn perennials into nutrient-dense foods such as meat and milk.

"The unnecessary trappings modern American agriculture hangs around cattle are remarkable in the extreme – ploughing, planting, combine harvesters, grain elevators, feedlots and anhydrous ammonia tanks. If we sat down with a committee to try and figure out how to make something needlessly complex and inefficient, the modern confinement, grain-based herbivore production model would be a perfect example.

"If we concentrate on nature's simplicity based on these three principles, grazing becomes the most environmentally-friendly food production model possible."

Decades before Salatin showed the enormous productivity of Virginia grasslands, scientists uncovered the reasons for the productive power of grazed pastures. Natural grasslands never contain just a single species. Wherever grasslands grow they contain perhaps dozens of species of grass, clovers and herbs. The precise mix of species in the grassland "community", as it's called, will depend on such factors as the soil type, the nature of the underlying rock, height above sea level, topography and climate.

The mix of species is never static. As environmental conditions change, so some species become more numerous at the expense of others. For example, a period of drought will result in the decline of some species, while others – such as deep-rooting, drought-resistant grasses and herbs – will strengthen their hold on the pasture community. The whole ecology of the pasture is in a constant state of flux.

When grazing animals spread their dung across a pasture they raise the fertility of the underlying soil. This encourages the more productive, faster growing grass species at the expense of slow-growing grasses. As productive species gradually become dominant in the pasture, the nutrition of the grazing animal improves. This means the animals excrete droppings that are more nutrient-rich, and this in turn ratchets up the fertility cycle of the soil.

So, properly managed, the whole grazing system becomes more and more productive. Without any artificial chemical inputs, food output of the land increases and consequently, so does the nutritional value of this food. Andre Voisin described it as an "organic spiral of production", which progressively enriches the soil and brings about a steady increase in the production from well-managed pastures.[9]

In Britain the art of efficient grazing has been the gateway to health and prosperity for generations of country people. For centuries village communities in the wild uplands in the west of the country followed the custom of taking their cattle up to the "shielings", the mountain grazings, during the summer months. The shieling system - part of a livestock-herding culture dating back to Neolithic times – was widely practised in high country right across Europe, and still survives today in parts of Norway, Sweden and the Alps.[10]

The seasonal use of mountain pastures meant that more cattle could be kept than the main holding alone would support. Each year part of the village community, (often the girls and young women), would live in rudimentary huts high in the hills, close to the upland grazings. There they would pass the summer months milking the cows, and making the butter and cheese that would help sustain their families through the winter.

In the autumn the animals would be returned to the village where they would spend the winter on the lowland pastures, or be fed on hay and root crops such as turnips and swedes. Surplus animals could be slaughtered and their meat salted down, or handed over to drovers for sale in the markets of the south and east.

The presence of grazing animals trampling and dunging on the turf during the summer gradually improved the pasture, making it more productive year by year. The young women herders were skilled at knowing exactly when to move their cattle off one stretch of grass and on to the next. As a result, they were able to produce large amounts of food from terrain that today would be considered harsh and unproductive.

There are good grounds for thinking the meat and milk produced on the shielings were rich in vitamins and protective fats. Certainly the villagers themselves were convinced that butter they made on the summer pastures was better-tasting and healthier than that produced on the lowlands.

Today the art of grazing has been largely lost. Few farmers believe grassland alone can produce much food, and certainly not without massive applications of chemical nitrate fertilizer. For the most part livestock farmers prefer to feed their animals on grains and industrial crops like maize. However costly and inefficient this kind of farming may be, it is at least predictable and measurable. For a given amount of feed energy you can, up to a point, predict the output of meat and milk you'll get in return.

Most farmers consider grass to be useful for "a bit of keep", or even as a "maintenance" ration for their animals. But the idea that it might produce large amounts of healthy meat and milk leaves them sceptical. Yet if they were prepared to put the same management effort into grazing pastures that they currently invest in the growing of industrial grains, they'd find they could produce better food at lower cost.

American farmers are equally ignorant of the productive power of grazed grass. This is revealed in a popular phrase for grazing land – "the back-forty". The term is used for any run-down patch of pasture where livestock are shut up in spring, and from where the survivors are collected in autumn. If most are still alive by then, farmers congratulate themselves on a job well done. With luck a few animals might actually have put on some weight. But no one expects much more from grass.

Joel Salatin and a few other pioneer graziers are proving, not merely that pastures can be productive, but that they are the only eco-friendly way of producing large amounts of food. Likewise in Britain, a group of "free-range" milk producers are discovering that the young women who ran their cattle on the summer shielings knew a thing or two about producing healthy foods.

A new generation of graziers has found that by mimicking the grazing cycles of the great natural grasslands, they can produce large amounts of beef and milk at low cost and in ways that benefit the environment. And, as we've seen, the foods from grass are invariably healthy.

In the east Cornwall town of Launceston there's a renowned butcher's shop called P. Warren and Son. They specialise in high quality meat from traditional British breeds. Whenever I'm driving that way I invariably call in and buy something to take home.

The firm runs its own farms, and I was delighted to see that they described themselves as "graziers" as well as butchers. It told me all I needed to know about their delicious meat.

7

Free range milk

Tom and Tara Morris run a dairy herd on a beautiful grassland farm at the edge of the Quantock Hills. The tall, thick hedges ring to the sound of songbirds, and in summer the fields are bright with the flowers of clover. Even in this attractive part of the west country East Lydeard Farm looks special.

There's something else remarkable about this farm. The dairy cows stay out on their lush, green pastures pretty well all year round. They're as close to being "free range" as you're ever likely to find in Britain.

This might not seem unusual. We're used to seeing cows grazing placidly in the fields. But impressions can be deceiving. Most of Britain's high-yielding dairy cows spend many months confined to sheds. Equally important, for much of the year they're fed rations that don't include their natural feed – fresh grass.

Instead they're fed silage, a form of pickled grass, grown with large amounts of chemical fertilizer and harvested by large machines of the sort grain-growers go in for. Maize silage, an industrial crop, is another favourite with today's intensive dairy farmers. On top of these oil-dependent forage crops there's likely to be a hefty dollop of cereals. Today's high yielding dairy cows are fed as much as three tonnes of the stuff each year.

Farmers are able to calculate, from the feeds they give their cows, how much milk comes from each dietary constituent. On many of today's intensive dairy herds the proportion of milk from grazed pasture can be as little as 10 per cent or even less. This is bad news for those of us who drink milk and eat dairy foods. It means that most of them won't deliver the health benefits we'd get from the milk of pasture-fed cows.

At East Lydeard Farm, Tom Morris feeds a small amount of cereals to the herd. He also makes a little silage, principally to use up the inevitable surplus of grass that occurs in spring. But grazed grass makes up by far the biggest part of the cows' diet. The calculations show that no less than 80 per cent of their milk comes from grass. This means that it'll be rich in health-protecting vitamins and unsaturated fats including omega-3s and CLA.

Though the yields per cow are lower than on most intensive dairy farms, the costs are lower, too. The Morrises don't need expensive buildings or large, sophisticated machinery. The farm is organic so they don't buy chemical fertilizers. Instead they use clover and composted manure to maintain soil fertility. And on their grass-based diet the cows stay healthy and fertile, so the vet's bills are next to zero. All in all it adds up to a very profitable enterprise despite the comparatively low yields.

A modern intensive herd, fed a full range of high-input forage crops and cereals, can easily achieve an average yield of 8,000 litres a cow or more. The East Lydeard Farm herd produces not much more than half that. Yet it makes a good deal more profit. The 180 cows support three families, Tom and Tara Morris, plus the families of their two herdsmen – no mean achievement on a farm of just 150 hectares. The benefits to the community as a whole are even more impressive.

By relying on solar-powered pastures rather than oil-powered crops to feed the cows, the farm represents a sustainable, reliable source of food. Whatever happens to oil prices, however scarce chemical fertilizers become, this Somerset farm will go on delivering the healthiest milk around.

With high levels of organic matter in the soil, it will also withstand periods of drought or spells of torrential rain. In short, it's about as secure against climate change as any food system can be. And since there's good money in it for the farmer, it's hard to understand why all British dairy farms aren't run this way.

Over coffee in the farm kitchen, Tom gave me his theory on why fewer than one-in-ten dairy farmers produce milk from pasture. It's essentially because most farmers are scared of grass, as he put it. Although this sounded odd, I knew what he meant.

Grazing is a kind of alchemy. If you get it right, it's as if you're producing gold from base metal. Get it wrong, however, and the output can be unpredictable. This is why most farmers stick with the expensive, oil-based system they know. It may be costly, wasteful and barely profitable, but it produces a lot of milk. Therefore it's assumed to be superior.

The art of grazing – knowing when to take animals on and off a pasture – has been practiced by country people for generations. Today there's a new bit of kit to make it easier. It's known as the electric fence. Well maybe it's not that new. In fact it's been around on farms since the 1950s. But today's pasture farmers are discovering that it's the key to making use of the seemingly limitless solar-powered potential of grassland.

The most important decision of Tom Morris's working day is estimating how far to move the electric fence. Twice a day the cows must be allowed a fresh patch of pasture. Tom judges by eye how much fresh turf to allow the herd. It's a fine judgement that takes account of the height of the grass and how thick the crop is.

Some grassland farmers use special tools to measure the amount of grass available. I once helped develop one of them during my time as a post-graduate student in north Wales. The device went by the fancy name of "capacitance plate meter". Basically it was a flat metal plate with a dozen or so spikes sticking out of it. You put the plate in the grass with the spikes down, and a battery powered meter on the top measured the electrical resistance between them. This gave you a measure of the bulk density of the grass sward.

A simpler device used by many farmers today is known as the "sward stick". It provides an instant estimate of the amount of feed available in a patch of grass.

Tom Morris uses neither of these technical aids. He relies on his own eye and judgement, based on experience gained over a working lifetime on this farm. He knows every field and the pastures in it. That's what makes his grazing decisions unerringly accurate. The proof is in the sheer productivity of the farm and the fact that it makes good profits, even during times considered tough by most dairy farmers.

The art of grazing – or "grassmanship" as it used to be called – was once widely known in the British countryside. Throughout history grass has been the nation's most important crop, its greatest wealth creator. Down the ages the skill of managing grazing pastures was handed on from generation to generation among country people.

As recently as the mid 1960s I saw it widely practised on the hill farms of north Wales. At that time, having to plough up and re-sow a worn-out pasture was seen as an admission of failure – a sign that the farmer had mismanaged the grazing by allowing weeds to become dominant or by letting cattle damage the turf by trampling or "poaching" it.

What changed this time-honoured culture was chemical fertilizer, particularly nitrates. Sold heavily in the 1960s and 70s by the chemical companies and the government's own farm advisers, nitrate fertilizers took away the need for grazing skills. Throw a bit of nitrogen fertilizer on a pasture and the grass grows, farmers discovered, particularly when the traditional, flower-rich grassland was replaced with a monoculture of perennial ryegrass.

No longer was there any need to look after the clovers in their pastures. Nor did they have to worry about soil organic matter. Nitrate fertilizer would keep the grass growing.

For fifty years livestock farmers have heaped nitrate fertilizers on their grassland. It still produces grass of sorts. But it's grass depleted of trace elements and sometimes made sour by mineral imbalance. This is why dairy farmers have to spend large sums of money on mineral supplements for their cows. Like vitamin supplements for human beings, they're a lot less affective than feeding nutrient-rich foods.

Even so, it's grass of a kind. But the nitrates used to grow it will have cost the farmer dear, particularly as fertilizer prices follow the oil price into the stratosphere. They'll have cost the rest of us a polluted planet and foods stripped of their health-giving nutrients.

Since turning their backs on grazing and becoming dependent on oil, dairy farmers have acquired a number of other expensive habits. The maize, soya and cereal grains they now routinely feed to their animals are all grown with costly oil. The cost to their animals is ill health and shortened lives.

Grassland farmers like Tom and Tara incur few of these costs. If all British farmers were to make full use of our great grassland resource we would all benefit. We'd enjoy healthier foods and a diverse, less-polluted countryside.

On the international scene, Britain would be reinstated to its rightful place as one of the world's top grass-farming nations. Because of our climate and soils, this country has a great natural advantage in producing foods from grass. In a free-trading economy, where products are made at the locations best suited to them, the products of grass ought to be pouring off British farms.

Tom Phillips, the New Zealand agriculturalist now working as a consultant in the UK, helps British farmers make use of this under-used resource. He's convinced the potential for growing foods this way is huge. It could mean lower food prices and a healthier diet for consumers, he maintains, plus lower costs and healthier profits for farmers. Sadly Phillips's view is that the country has a long way to go. In fact in its use of this natural resource, Britain could be regarded almost as a developing country.

Coming from a New Zealander this is a valid criticism. New Zealand farmers are the world leaders in grassland farming, and have been for many years. I remember in my student days two-thirds of the scientific research papers on grasslands and their exploitation came out of that country.

New Zealand grassland – rich in clover – is grazed all year round and the country's livestock production is powered principally by the sun. Products such as butter and lamb can be shipped to Britain from the other side of the world and still appear on supermarket shelves with a lower carbon footprint than the same foods intensively-farmed at home.

The promoters of Anchor butter, for years Britain's best known brand, make great play of the fact that it comes from "free-range cows". The UK dairy industry became very annoyed about this claim and complained about it to the Advertising Standards Authority. What right had the New Zealanders to use the emotive term "free-range" for their cows?

But when the Anchor marketing people explained the facts of New Zealand dairy farming, the ASA rejected the complaint. They ruled that the marketing executives at Anchor had every right to use the phrase. Since this ruling I notice that the Anchor butter wrapper has been redesigned. Last time I looked there were little tufts of grass all over it to emphasise its pastoral origins.

So the comment from a New Zealander that Britain could be making far better use of grasslands is worth taking to heart. The dairy sector, in particular, is in a dire state principally because it has shifted its production base from solar energy and grassland to oil and chemically-grown annual crops.

Most dairy farmers throw far too much nitrate fertilizer onto their grassland monocultures. Every tonne of fertilizer nitrogen equates to more than six tonnes of carbon dioxide released into the atmosphere.

You don't have to be an organic supporter to recognise that the way nitrates are used on many dairy farms is both wasteful and environmentally damaging. Farmers measure fertilizer rates in kilograms applied per hectare of grassland. Some intensive dairy farmers apply as much as 450kg a hectare every year. The cost can easily add up to £60,000 or more.

By any standards this is ludicrous. Clovers, like those that fill the pastures at East Lydeard Farm, could be supplying the equivalent of 120kg for free. That's the amount of nitrogen "fixed" from the air by the nodules in clover plant roots. On top of this there are the nitrates produced naturally by free-living microbes in a fertile, biologically active soil. Together they can produce another 100kg of nitrate equivalent.

Even without going organic, every one of Britain's fertilizer-profligate farmers could reduce their level of nitrates by half without losing any production. As an organic farmer Tom Morris uses no nitrate fertilizer at all, yet he still manages to achieve a reasonable – and highly profitable - output.

Then there's the question of all the industrial grains British dairy farmers rely on:- cereals, soya, maize and the like. All these are produced expensively with chemical fertilizers and sprays, and many are imported. All cause sickness in the animals they're fed to and may well be responsible for ill health in the people who consume the products. Most would be unnecessary if farmers learned to use their pastures properly.

On their unnatural diets the modern, intensively-farmed dairy cow is one of the most unhealthy animals on the planet. Too many starchy grains in the rumen increase the acidity in this large, fermentation chamber. The rumen microbes react by producing an excess of lactic acid, some of which is absorbed into the bloodstream where it plays havoc with the animal's normal metabolism.

Toxins are released into the bloodstream. These are produced by the decay of micro-organisms killed off in the over-acid conditions. Dangerous pathogens take their place, seizing the new opportunity and multiplying rapidly. This is why high-yielding, grain fed cows are beset with ill-health.

Disease is endemic in Britain's dairy industry. Infections of the udder occur at an annual rate of seventy cases in every hundred cows, according to one university survey.[1] Routine antibiotic treatments are used during the "dry" period – the few short weeks of the year when cows are not lactating. But these deal with the symptoms, not the cause of disease. Cows are sick because of the way they're fed and managed.

As many as one-quarter of the national herd suffer from lameness, commonly caused by a restriction in the blood supply to the feet. This is caused by toxins and histamines in the blood, the result of over-acidic conditions in the rumen. As if this weren't enough, the stresses on these high-performing cows have led to a rising tide of infertility.

Many of today's intensive dairy cows are worn out by the

time they've reached their third lactation cycle. By contrast, cows grazing naturally on clover-rich pastures for much of the year – like the cows at East Lydeard Farm – can stay productive for ten years or more.

Together the costs of fertilizers, big machines, diesel fuel, purchased grains and the sickness they cause add a huge cost burden to modern dairy farming. That's why today's dairy farmers struggle to make a living, even at milk prices that are historically high. Their businesses are weighed down with unnecessary costs.

What this means is we could all be drinking healthier milk, from healthy cows, at a price below what we're paying today. It sounds like – and is – a shocking indictment of modern intensive farming. What's even more disturbing is the fact that the way to produce cheap, nutritious milk was established more than eighty years ago and subsequently hushed up by the dairy industry.

In 1920, as British agriculture slid towards recession, a farmer-engineer called Arthur Hosier bought a large expanse of run-down pasture-land on the chalk downs near Marlborough.

It was a scrubby, gorse-infested patch of ground and he got it for just £5 an acre. Even so his farming friends thought he'd gone off his head. At that time farm prices were heading downwards following a short term "mini-boom" during World War One. Many farmers were finding it hard enough to make a profit on good land, never mind the thin, worn-out soils of the chalk downs.

When Hosier's friends heard what he was planning to do with his new estate they were even more alarmed. His idea was to cover the wind-swept, scrubby grassland with dairy cows and start selling "outdoor milk".

To farmers of the time producing milk seemed a great way to lose money. Cheap imports from New Zealand and Denmark had undermined the market for farmhouse butter and cheese. The milk price, which reached the dizzy heights of 2s. and 6d. a gallon during the war, had since collapsed. In London milk was selling for as little as 6d. And the quality of the stuff was dire.

A few years earlier the National Clean Milk Society had made the astonishing discovery that the average sample of milk sold in the capital contained a higher concentration of bacteria than raw sewage at a Birmingham sewage farm. This was a major reason for an appalling death rate among London's infants. The numbers of children dying before they reached their first birthday was double that of British soldiers killed in the first year of the Great War.

On his new Wiltshire estate, Arthur Hosier pledged to produce milk so pure and nutritious that it would transform the health of people in Britain's grimy industrial towns. What's more he would produce it so cheaply that this "super-milk" would be affordable to even the poorest families.[2]

Hosier was as good as his word. For five years the local health authority sampled his milk and checked it for pathogens – disease-causing bacteria. Finally they pronounced it among the purest in Britain. In fact it was regularly found to be completely free of coliform bacteria, a level of purity few dairy farmers would be able to match today. So clean and nutritious was the milk that it was supplied to London hospitals for people too ill to risk any additional challenge to their immune systems.

Hosier's revolutionary idea was to keep his cows out on pasture all the year round. Most dairy farmers housed and milked their cows in over-crowded sheds, at least during the winter months. In these damp, poorly-ventilated buildings conditions were ideal for the spread of disease.

Hygiene standards were woeful. Dairy staff with manure-stained hands would milk into open pails. Sterilization of equipment was unheard of. Though milk was sterile when secreted by the cow's mammary tissue, it was anything but sterile by the time it had been in the churn for a few hours.

Hosier changed everything. He believed that by keeping his cows out in the fresh air – in "sanatorium conditions" as he called them - on a natural diet of grass and hay, they would remain healthy and free from disease. This would mean that the milk they produced would be pure and nutritious.

At the heart of his system was a portable milking unit built to his own design. It was a sort of shed on wheels that could be shifted by tractor to a fresh bit of pasture every day. Big enough to accommodate six cows at a time, it was, in essence, a mobile milking parlour.

A converted shepherd's hut was used to house the petrol engine and vacuum pump of the milking machine, a boiler producing hot water for cleaning and sterilizing equipment, a dynamo for lighting and a refrigeration unit for cooling the milk. The whole system was designed to ensure milk never came into contact with the air. It passed along nickel-plated pipes, through the cooler, to an airtight and insulated tank so it remained virtually sterile.

Though the run-down estate was cold and exposed, the cows were expected to stay out on pasture all year round in all weathers. Despite the climate they remained remarkably healthy under their "free-range conditions", quickly adapting to the outdoor life by growing long, thick coats. At the same time they stayed free of the crippling ailments that plague modern dairy farms – lameness, infertility and udder disease.

They didn't seem to contract tuberculosis either. In the 1920s TB was rife in the human population, with tens of thousands dying from it every year. Many were believed to contract the disease from contaminated milk. This disturbing fact was one of the main drivers behind the health authority campaign to get compulsory pasteurization – heat treatment - introduced for all milk.

But in their "sanatorium" conditions Hosier's cows never developed TB. He was convinced the disease was spread by crowding cattle together in warm buildings and unsanitary yards. At Wexcombe cows stayed disease-free and healthy. Even "reactors", (cattle giving a positive result in TB tests), failed to develop the disease when brought on to the farm. He claimed: "If all cows were kept in the open air on dry land and properly fed, tuberculosis would be non-existent in five years."

Today in Britain's dairy industry, where cows are routinely crowded into sheds and given "unnatural" feeds, TB is once again on the march. At the end of 2007 more than five thousand cattle herds were under TB restriction. Farmers blame the badger population for infecting their cows and are pressing the government to exterminate badgers in the most infected areas. Hosier showed that when cows are kept in healthy conditions and fed on grass and hay, they don't get infected.

In 1927, as the bread queues lengthened across recession-hit Britain, Hosier stood up at the Farmers' Club in London's

Whitehall Place to report on his new system.[3] His audience of large farmers and landowners were eager to hear of any innovative way to turn a profit in those stricken times. Hosier told them there was good money to be made, even at a time of recession, by producing a high quality food and selling direct to the public.

He'd been able to run his outdoor herds with just half the labour needed for conventionally housed cattle, he told them.

But it was the health of his animals – and the purity of the milk they produced – that interested him most. Beside him on the platform sat the public health officer responsible for his milk, a Mr C E Tangye, the county medical officer for Wiltshire. The health chief explained that he and his staff regularly sampled the milk of Wexcombe together with that of dozens of other dairy farms in the county.

The results showed that much of Wiltshire's milk supply was so contaminated with bacteria that it was "fit only to be pasteurized". But not so the milk of the Hosier open-air system. It was, in Mr Tangye's own words, "100 per cent pure".

The health chief was in no doubt that this method of producing milk was the best system for Britain. He told the meeting: "From the public health point of view the economical production of milk as demonstrated by Mr Hosier places his system far ahead of all the others. This is because his milk is for everyone and not just the favoured few."

Over the next few years a small number of farmers adopted the system. By 1930 a total of eighty-six had taken up "open air" dairying, producing between them enough milk to supply a city the size of Leicester. Two years later a team of economists from Oxford

University carried out a study of over seventy open-air herds. They concluded that in many parts of Britain the future of dairy farming lay in the adoption of these simple, open-air methods.

Had Hosier's revolution continued we'd all now be enjoying a wonderful, health-giving food. Unlike today's milk it was so pure it didn't need heat treatment to make it safe. This meant it retained its full complement of nutrients, including vitamins, enzymes and protective fatty-acids. It would have helped prevent many of today's most crippling ailments – heart disease, many cancers, osteoporosis, arthritis and asthma.

Sadly it wasn't to be. The big dairy companies convinced the government that the only safe milk was milk that had been pasteurized. In effect this meant farmers could no longer sell their milk direct to the public, no matter how pure it was. Instead it would have to go to one of the dairy companies for heat treatment. The dairy industry had effectively taken control of the nation's milk supply.

Despite the clear health benefits of pasture-fed milk, dairy farming has since gone in precisely the wrong direction. Herds have got bigger and cows have been concentrated in ever larger numbers inside sheds, where they're fed diets containing large amounts of industrial grain.

It's virtually impossible to buy healthy milk in today's supermarkets or, for that matter, from the home delivery floats of the major dairy companies. It's true there are still a handful of pasture-fed herds dotted around the British countryside. But inside the stainless steel silos of the dairy companies, this good milk is swamped in the deluge from farms that fill their cows with cereal grains and soya. Even the so-called healthy milks are spoiled by the standards of their poorest producers.

Organic milk, for example, is a blend of the good and the not-so-good. Organic standards require that at least 60 per cent of the ration must be in the form of grass and forage. In terms of its nutrient content, milk produced to this minimum standard won't compare in quality with milk of cows getting 80 per cent of their feed in the form of grazed pasture, organic or not. And, as on conventional farms, milk produced to higher standards will be diluted with milk produced to the bare minimum standard.

I did a tour of my local Sainsburys store to see what kind of milks were on offer. I counted more than twenty brands including organic, omega-3 enriched, filtered and Jersey milks. But what I would judge to be the healthiest milk around – "free range", pasture-fed milk – was not to be found. We're offered what looks like a wide choice. However, the best, and what ought to be the cheapest, is not available.

In the United States it's a different story. While healthy, pasture-fed milk may have been forgotten in Britain it's acquiring new enthusiasts across the US. Among its producers is Mark McAfee, who, as we've seen, runs Organic Pastures Dairy Company (OPDC) in California's fertile San Joaquin Valley.[4]

Like Arthur Hosier's cows more than eighty years earlier, Mark's herd stays out on pasture all year round. And like Hosier's cows they're milked through a mobile milking parlour that's frequently towed to a new location. As in Britain, this way of managing cows produces milk of superb quality and purity.

Naturopathic doctor Ron Schmid, whose book The Untold

Story of Milk has been influential in the development of pasture-fed dairy foods in the US, explains that when people drink this healthy, raw milk their own intestines become populated with beneficial bacteria.[5] This is one reason why people regularly drinking raw milk have been shown to have a higher resistance to pathogenic organisms.

It's a view shared by McAfee. Western industrial diets have weakened the immune systems of most Americans, he argues. Many of us now have little choice but to eat the "sterile" products of the food industry. Our bodies are unable to tolerate the natural "living" foods that evolution prepared us for. People with poor immunity can become ill by eating even small amounts of foreign bacteria their bodies are unfamiliar with.

He explains: "It's estimated that 70 per cent of the strength of a healthy immune system depends on the diversity of the living bacteria in the human gut. Raw milk provides a perfect source for the 'seeding and feeding' of these living populations of bacteria. Consuming raw milk and dairy products is an important step towards regaining immune strength and overall good health."

He's unhappy that in the US most organic milk is pasteurized or even turned into UHT (ultra heat treated) milk. He considers heat treatment to be a denial of the essential quality of organic foods. "Organic" means diversity of life and soil. Heat treatment converts foods that are "living" into foods that are "dead". How can something that's dead be considered natural or organic, he wonders.

Though OPDC is California's first producer of organic, grass-fed, raw milk, farms producing this healthy food are now springing up across America. They're part of a movement called the Campaign for Real Milk, modelled on the successful British Campaign for Real Ale.

Some of the new producers are locked in battle with federal and state departments of food and agriculture. But since the food is daily picking up new enthusiasts, it's unlikely the authorities will succeed in getting them all shut down.

To many of the farmer pioneers of raw milk it's a simple question of freedom. In a free society has the state any right to deny people a natural, health-giving food that generations of their ancestors have enjoyed and thrived on?

In Britain the tradition of drinking milk from pasture-fed cows is older than our history. Long before the Norman conquest the people of village England were drinking the milk of cows grazed on the communal pastures. Until the mid 20th century milk from cows feeding principally on grass and other green forage crops was pretty well the only milk you could get.

Today this milk is unobtainable. At the very time food scientists are beginning to discover the health benefits of milk produced this way, there are precious few places where consumers can buy it. Instead Britain's dairy industry is locked into a system of production that's inefficient and which misuses resources.

Tom and Tara Morris, whose grass-fed organic milk must rank as one of the best in the country, sell to one of the major farmer-owned co-ops. At the milk factory it's bulked up with supplies from other organic farms, most of which won't rely so heavily on grazing. While all organic milk has more omega-3s and vitamins than the milk of intensive, non-organic herds, it won't be as nutrient-rich as the grass-fed version. All organic foods aren't the same.

Before I left East Lydeard Farm, I asked Tom to give me a call if ever he decided to start selling his wonderful milk direct from the farm. If he did, I told him, I'd be driving to his beautiful farm a couple of times a week to collect it. He advised me not to hold my breath. It was up to the milk co-ops and dairy companies to decide when free-range milk would be viable as a branded product.

The dairy companies must be aware of the health benefits of pasture-fed milk. They surely know of the new research linking grazing to protective fatty acids such as CLA? It's anyone's guess why they choose not to market this superb food.

Fortunately there are still a few family dairy farms producing and selling the real stuff. One of them is in the small Buckinghamshire village of North Crawley, just a few miles from Newport Pagnell. The sign on the wall of the old, redbrick dairy building says G Adderson and Sons, Dairymen and Farmers. Running the enterprise are Gordon and Beryl Adderson and their two sons Gary and Ricky. Norman Adderson, Gordon's father, founded the business back in the 1930s.

While Gary looks after the sixty or so cows, Gordon and Ricky deliver their milk to hundreds of homes in the surrounding villages. This means that milk produced on these lush, green pastures has been providing a wonderful, healthy food to the locals for around eighty years. Far more than a local food, it's a local treasure.

I called at the farm on a bright, showery day in late July. I'd seen it mentioned on a website listing sources of unpasteurised milk. The brief description whetted my appetite. Referring to the cows' diet it simply said they were grass-fed in summer and given home-made silage in winter. This sounded promising so I thought I'd pay them a visit.

As I walked with Gary to get the cows in for afternoon milking, it didn't take long to realise that this was a farm dedicated to producing the highest quality milk. The fields - most of which were fairly small – were all down to species-rich pasture, much of it filled with clover.

The tall, thick hedges, many dating back to the middle ages, contained species like buckthorn, sallow, bullace and dogwood, along with the more common blackthorn, oak and field maple. For grazing animals there was plenty of botanical diversity here to ensure a nutrient-rich diet, which would hopefully translate into healthy milk for the customers.

The cows were rather special, too. These were no highly-bred milk machines, genetically-programmed to turn out large volumes of white liquid. Many of them were crosses between black-and-white Friesians and other breeds, such as the Jersey and more recently the French Montbeliard, the cow whose milk makes the famous Comte cheese.

Gary breeds all his own herd replacements. No cattle are ever bought in at Lodge Farm. The aim is to minimise the risk of disease in the herd. For obvious reasons it's something farmers selling direct to consumers are usually more careful about than those producing anonymous "commodities" for far off markets.

Gary has two main aims. He tries to breed animals that will thrive on pasture and remain productive for many years. By and large these are attributes of the traditional breeds. On their clover-rich pastures the cows stay healthy and productive for twelve years or more.

He's also striving for cows that will produce high quality milk rather than large amounts of indifferent white liquid. There's a small pasteuriser on the farm allowing the family partners to sell both heat-treated and untreated milk. Regular customers love the taste of their local, pasture-fed milk. Many more travel considerable distances to buy untreated milk at the farm shop.

In fact, this section of their market has increased in recent years, says Gary, as people discover the health benefits of untreated milk as a whole, natural food. One woman regularly visits the farm from forty miles away simply to buy untreated milk. Before discovering it she was intolerant to milk. But on Lodge Farm's unpasteurised milk her intolerance has disappeared.

Because the farm sells untreated milk, it is subjected to frequent and unannounced inspections by the Food Standards Agency. The herd also has to undergo more frequent tests for bovine TB than dairy farms selling milk for pasteurisation. Gary has no worries about this. Since the farm began retailing untreated, pasture-fed milk back in the 1930s there has never been a health problem.

In a world of ever bigger factory farms, traditional family farms like this are rare gems. So are the nutritious, healthy foods they produce. Though Lodge Farm milk may cost a few pence more than supermarket milk, as a food it's incomparably better. In terms of the nutrients and improved health it delivers, it also represents good value for money.

There are still a scattering of dairy farms like this around Britain. For those involved it's not an easy life. Gary Adderson milks his cows twice every day, seven days a week, fifty-two weeks a year. He hasn't had a holiday in seven years. It's a job and a way of life he clearly loves. But if we value family farms and the foods they produce, we have to secure them by seeking out and buying their products.

For the sake of our health – and for the health of the countryside – there's a strong argument, not merely for protecting farms like this, but for opening up new ones across the length and breadth of Britain. What could be better for the nation's health and wealth than the proliferation of family-run dairy farms selling high-quality milk to their local communities?

It has happened before in this nation's glorious agrarian history. We can make it happen again.

8

Green and pleasant land

The grass fields I remember from childhood were noisy places. There were a number of them just a few minutes from our road on a north Reading council estate. As kids we'd spend hours there in summer, re-enacting World War Two or the shoot-out from High Noon. It was the kind of landscape you don't see any more – small fields, straggling hedges and brambles. To the modern, profit-minded farmer it would look like a waste of space. There'd be a dozens of different grasses, clovers and wild flowers, including buttercups, cowslips and a whole lot more I couldn't identify. Sometimes there would be a bunch of heifers or bullocks grazing placidly or quietly chewing the cud in the shade of the hedgerow elm.

Even to a ten-year-old it seemed a peaceful sort of place – until you sat down on the turf and listened, that is. Then, it seemed, all hell had been let loose. The grass sward was filled with sounds - a hissing, buzzing, clicking, scraping cacophony of noise. Things would start landing on you, scurrying across you or flying by you. There would be the recognisable stuff such as grasshoppers large and small, brown and green and yellow, – beetles, ladybirds, hover-flies and flickering butterflies in a variety of colours. There would also be a host of nameless bugs, spiders and flying creatures with long legs and dangerous looking mouthparts. Some would look so fearsome that you'd jump up in horror, brushing frantically at your bare arms and legs, convinced you'd narrowly escaped a lethal bite from a venomous species your mum had failed to warn you about. Down there at insect level everything was noise, movement and conflict. In those far off days of the 1950s the life of the grass field provided a summer soundtrack to playtime, even for urban youngsters. But not any more.

I was back in a grass field not long ago. It was on a modern intensive dairy farm, just before the milk price shot up. The farmer had decided to give up milk production, and I was having a look round before the two hundred or so black-and-white cows went under the auctioneer's hammer. As I walked over the pasture fields, the contrast with those I'd remembered from childhood could hardly have been greater. For a start there was only one grass species present. Unfortunately I knew it only too well – perennial ryegrass, the fertilizer manufacturer's friend. And, unlike the tough, mixed-species turf of old, this one was soft and "open".

When you looked closely it was clear each individual grass plant was distinct and separate, surrounded by a tiny patch of bare earth. This modern pasture was like the pixels on a computer screen – a million individual plants growing on a soil that was soft and exposed. Dosed with enough chemical fertilizer, no doubt it produced thick crops of nitrate-filled silage. But robbed of its microbial life the soil structure had gone. A rain storm in summer would have run off it as if it were concrete, while winter rain would have sat on top in waterlogged pools. But to me there was one, over-riding difference. Even when you got close to this turf it was utterly silent. Though this was summer there was no rasp of grasshopper, no hum of bee. The field was lifeless. There are tens of thousands of fields like this up and down the country.

Because there's still plenty of grassland about, particularly on the western side of Britain – and because most of it remains obdurately green – we believe this part of the country, at least, is healthy and flourishing. When we watch the sprayers trundling up and down arable fields through the spring and summer, we're deceived into thinking it's crop areas that have suffered most from chemical farming. Unfortunately this is far from the truth. Weedkillers and chemical fertilizers have turned grassland into "green deserts" too.

Britain's native grassland plants are the ones that occupied much of lowland Britain at the end of the Ice Age. As forest cover gradually spread across the land, these plants of the open ground were restricted to woodland clearings. Then, during the Neolithic period, human beings began clearing the forests. Grassland plants quickly occupied the newly opened ground. Species such as burnet, bird's-foot trefoil, meadow saxifrage, sorrel, violet, rock rose, gentian, stitchwort, violet and hay rattle have all been traced back to the late glacial period.[1]

Under traditional management these semi-natural grasslands were mostly grazed or cut for hay. The only inputs were animal manure and sometimes lime or "marl", a lime-rich clay. This kind of management – interacting with natural variation in climate, soil type and topography – produced "communities" of plants that were distinct and characteristic of the place they grew.

The combination of grasses and non-grass plants on an area of southern chalk downland, for example, would be very different from those found on wet, acidic soils on the Pennines. But what these grasslands had in common was that they all contained many different species - perhaps dozens. Each had its own associated fauna, from microbes to insects, and on up the food chain to birds and mammals. This is why Britain's grasslands once made such a big contribution to the wildlife and biodiversity of these islands, perhaps dozens

The richest mix of plant species is usually found on soils where the parent rock is chalk or limestone. Not surprisingly these habitats attract calcium-loving species. On the southern chalk downlands the dominant grasses are likely to be the fine-leaved sheep's fescue and red fescue, or the more fibrous upright brome or tor grass. But there will also be a host of flowering plants to fill the turf with colour through the summer.

These could include cowslips, kidney vetch, yellow rock-rose, the purple clustered bellflower, small scabious and pale fairy flax. In the limestone areas of Derbyshire, Yorkshire and Cumbria the grasslands are dominated by blue moorgrass. But they also contain species like slender bedstraw, wild thyme, rock-rose and eyebright.

Soils that are more acid than those of chalk and limestone

attract calcifugous or lime-hating species. Among the grasses you'll often find common bentgrass or the graceful wavy hairgrass, sometimes growing in close proximity to purple flowering heather. The wild flowers associated with acid grasslands include wild gladiolus, with its startling crimson flowers, breckland thyme and the delicate, blue-flowered spring speedwell.

My own small grass field on Exmoor is officially described as "acid grassland", with its distinct species mix including meadow vetchling, selfheal, sweet vernal grass, pignut, meadow foxtail, salad burnet, burnet saxifrage and the yellow rough hawkbit.

Grasslands that are considered to be neither calcium-loving nor acid are said to be "neutral". These grasslands include the classic, flower-rich hay meadows of lowland Britain. Their dominant grass species is crested dogstail and their spectacular array of wild flowers include bright yellow rattle, common meadow rue, dyer's greenweed, meadow saxifrage, and the rare snake's head fritillary.

Whatever their individual make-up, Britain's flower-rich grasslands were once the glory of the countryside. Chalk grassland has long been famed for its rich mix of plant species – up to forty in a single square metre. But recent research has shown that acid and neutral grassland can contain at least as many grass and wild flower species.[2]

Tragically almost all have them have now been destroyed. Chemical fertilizers and weed-killers have taken a heavy toll. So has the campaign – driven by governments in close collaboration with the fertilizer companies – aimed at persuading farmers to abandon hay-making in favour of silage, a semi-industrial crop. EU subsidies for ploughing up grassland and growing cereals have also aided this grand theft of a rural treasure.

In 1984, as Europe groaned under the weight of subsidy-driven food mountains, only 3 per cent remained of the semi-natural grasslands that had occupied England and Wales fifty years earlier.[3] The destruction has continued ever since. What we're left with are a few tiny fragments that are today guarded and preserved like museum pieces.

What compounds the tragedy is the growing evidence that this widespread destruction was largely unnecessary. The chemical fertilizers that did so much of the damage supplied, on average, no more nitrogen than could have been produced by clovers and other legumes in grasslands, and in the crop rotations of mixed farming systems.

What's more, the foods produced by modern industrial methods are, as we've seen, nutritionally inferior to the foods raised on flower-rich pastures. As long ago as 1829 the writer J. L. Knapp described the quality of hay being made on the grasslands of the Severn Vale in Gloucestershire. He says: "The crop consists almost entirely of the common field scabious, loggerheads [knapweed], and the great ox-eye daisy. There is a scattering of bent, and here and there a specimen of the better grasses; but the predominant, staple of the crop, is scabious – it is emphatically a promiscuous herbage; yet on this rubbish do the cattle thrive, and from their milk is produced a cheese greatly esteemed for toasting."[4]

The benefits of species-rich grassland are equally clear today, though there are far fewer of them. Somerset farmers Will and Clare Barnard graze beef cows and their calves on the Pawlett Hams, a stretch of flat, low-lying grassland bordering the River Parrett, close to where it runs out into the Bristol Channel.

It's an empty, windswept sort of place. On a misty morning it's not hard to imagine the Kent marshes where Pip had his first frightening encounter with the convict Magwich in Charles Dickens' Great Expectations. For centuries "the Hams" have been renowned for producing tasty, succulent beef – the kind of beef that the wealthy merchants of Bristol would be happy to pay over the odds for. One of the principal reasons was that these low-lying, damp pastures contain a wealth of different species. Walking over the pastures today you'd see much the same mix of species that the graziers of Tudor England would have seen in the turf. Among the grasses are deep-rooting cocksfoot, with its ability to stay productive under wet or dry conditions, rough-stalked meadow grass, drought-resistant crested dogstail, and fragrant sweet vernal grass. The fertilizer manufacturer's favourite, perennial ryegrass, is present at a very low level.

Will's father Jim once commissioned a botanical survey of this section of the Hams. The survey found that there were thirty-three plant species growing on this one small area of flood plain. Among the grasses many wild flowers flourish. They include blue forget-me-not, the white-flowered mousear, tall ladies smock with its blush-pink blooms and red pimpernel. What's surprising about these flower-rich pastures is their capacity to produce nutritious food, as J. L. Knapp discovered. Will Barnard reports that after a summer season grazing the Hams, his cattle are virile, healthy and strong. The weight gains of the calves are "phenomenal", he says, more than double those of dairy calves raised on modern ryegrass monocultures.

The flower-rich pastures that produce such robust livestock are also beneficial for wild species. The lapwing, a bird once plentiful on British farmland, has been in decline for years, principally because of the decline of traditional grasslands. But on the Pawlett Hams the bird still flourishes, feeding as it does on the insects and grubs found in abundance on these damp pastures. Centuries of careful grazing has built up a rich store of fertility which powers – not just the flow of human foods – but the whole life of the land. It's the nature of life on this planet that all living things are connected. The decline of species here will have a knock-on effect elsewhere, perhaps in unpredictable ways. And nowhere are these interconnections more apparent than in grasslands.

In the 1980s, when subsidised, high-input agriculture was powering ahead, ornithologists started to notice a disturbing drop in the numbers of many farmland birds. Once common species such as the tree sparrow, bullfinch, song thrush, spotted flycatcher, linnet, lapwing and skylark had all gone into a steep decline. They were victims of neither disease nor climate change. They were the early casualties of the slow destruction of soil fertility.

Loss of humus and organic matter diminishes all the life of the land. The run-down begins with microscopic soil inhabitants – the protozoa, bacteria, fungi and algae that make up the base of the food chain. Next to be affected are the micro-fauna – the rotifers and nematodes living in the water films, and mites, springtails and small insects living in the soil air spaces. Then larger invertebrates go into a decline – the enchytraeid worms and earthworms, the millipedes and centipedes, the dipterous flies and the beetles.

Insect-eating birds are the next to be hit – lapwings, grey partridges, corncrakes and skylarks – along with small mammals, the shrews and voles. Finally the larger carnivores are affected, the stoats and weasels, the kestrels and barn owls. And so the landscape falls silent. The health of the entire countryside is sustained by the life of the soil, the ceaseless pulse of decay and renewal that beats in a fertile earth.

Species-rich grassland – with its power to build organic matter and fertility – is the source of this life. Particularly when it's closely linked to crop land, as in traditional mixed farming systems, it produces a countryside teeming with wildlife. What, I wonder, will future generations make of a society that cares so little for such a unique and valuable resource?

Grasslands and grazing are essential for the survival of many of Britain's most treasured wildlife species. Many butterflies, for example, depend on grasses to complete their life cycles. Species like the marbled white, the grayling, the meadow brown and the small heath lay their eggs directly on grasses, whose leaves later provide the food source for caterpillars.

Other species such as the orange tip, the small copper, the common blue and the brown argus require plants that are commonly found in flower-rich grasslands. One of the most extraordinary butterfly life cycles is that of the large blue, which lays its eggs on plants of wild thyme. The large blue is in danger of extinction, not least because of its bizarre adaptation. To survive its larvae must be carried by a red ant to an ants' nest, where they feed on ant grubs until they are ready to pupate.

Wet grassland – a habitat made up of species-rich grassland and marshy areas – is an important habitat for birds, especially wildfowl and waders. Among the rarer species that rely on this habitat for breeding are the snipe, redshank and shoveler, while over-wintering species include the wigeon, golden plover and Bewick's swan. Among the endangered bird species that depend on dry grassland are the stone curlew and the woodlark.

The wildlife value of most species-rich pasture depends on regular grazing. The grasses and herb species that make up the turf are adapted to the regular shearing off of their leaves, and to trampling and manuring. Without regular grazing, the botanical make-up of most pastures will slowly change through the process known as "succession", leading eventually to the "climax" vegetation. In most of Britain, without management our countryside would quickly become impassable scrubland and over many decades change into forest.

The need for grazing was often forgotten by early conservationists trying to save the surviving fragments of semi-natural grassland. When the first grassland nature reserves were set up, one of the first things many managers did was take away the cattle and sheep which had created the habitat in the first place.

These days we're a little smarter. It's now accepted that animals can play a crucial role in saving what's left of Britain's species-rich grasslands. A number of wildlife managers are choosing rare and regional breeds of livestock, such as Galloway or Highland cattle, for the job. This is because they're less selective in what they eat.

Modern cattle are likely to choose the most succulent grasses and vegetation to eat. This leads to a change in the composition of the turf with more aggressive grasses slowly taking over. By contrast the older livestock breeds are more likely to eat everything – brambles, grasses, herbs, the lot. So long as they're not allowed to crop the vegetation too short, this sort of grazing pattern protects the rich botanical make-up of the pasture.

While nature reserves may help semi-natural grasslands to survive as museum pieces, they won't go far in restoring wildlife to the countryside at large. Something rather more ambitious will be required. And for that to happen, we as citizens and consumers are going to have to take the lead. There's precious little chance of the politicians taking action to restore Britain's grassland heritage.

At the moment the government supports farmland biodiversity under its EU-funded agri-environment schemes, the most important of which is known as Environmental Stewardship. Farmers are paid so much per hectare for creating or maintaining bits of natural habitat on their land. These can include species-rich grassland.

The principal weakness of this approach is that it creates small islands of habitat in an ocean of hostile, commercial agriculture. It's very popular with intensive arable farmers, at least it was until commodity prices went through the roof. At today's grain prices there are plenty of large farmers who'd happily tear up their habitat management agreements and farm flat out for maximum yields right up to the boundary fence.

However, before the recent upturn it did give them an additional income stream in return for "greening up" marginal areas of the farm that had never been particularly profitable for crop growing. An area of land where the soil was poor, for example, might be allowed to revert to species rich grassland by natural regeneration from seeds lying dormant in the soil. So long as it was managed in a way that maintained the mixed-species character of the new grass, that land would go on attracting an annual payment from the taxpayer.

While such schemes make some contribution to the nation's wildlife stock, it's strictly limited. Species-rich grasslands were once enmeshed in Britain's farming culture. They were part of a sustainable system for producing food and managing the land. They were protected by being underpinned by the local economy and a way of life.

Today's pick-and-mix, portion-controlled habitats are often little more than window dressing. They're too small and too fragmented to restore Britain's lost wildlife. They're bolted onto a farming system that's basically hostile to them, and when the subsidies run out they'll disappear as fast as they were created.

A more cost effective way for governments to encourage biodiversity would be to concentrate the money on those few farms that are still run on traditional mixed-farming and organic principles. Their survival is threatened by the market dominance of large industrial grain producers. But as those farms drop out, the consequential loss to our wildlife can't be remedied by a few add-on habitats bought from the big arable farmers who take over.

One of the finest pasture farms I know is run by a brother and sister team, Richard and Rosamund Young, on the northern edge of the Cotswold Hills. Cattle grazing the flower-rich pastures at Kite's Nest Farm near Broadway in Worcestershire are as close to being genuinely free range as any I've seen. With the exception of fields "shut up" for hay, the animals are allowed to wander at will across more than a hundred hectares of grassland.

This gives them a good deal of choice over what they eat. It means they can select the plants that they know instinctively will give them the balance of nutrients they need. While this style of "extensive grazing" doesn't provide the food output of rotational paddocks, it's probably kindest to the animals.

The Youngs apply no chemical fertilizers or sprays to their grasslands. Their farm is totally organic. The beef herd has been "self contained" since the 1970s. No animals are bought in – all the beef cattle were born on the farm. There they live in family groups, each calf remaining with its mother until she weans it naturally when her milk dries up, about a month before the next calf is due. Even then the calf remains with the family group.

The beef produced so carefully at Kite's Nest Farm is sold from the little shop in the mellow stone farmhouse. Customers who know the meat come back time and time again, many of them travelling considerable distances to get it. They've found the beef to be unbeatable for flavour. Having tasted it, few want to go back to conventionally-raised meat.

But the Youngs produce a lot more than healthy beef at Kite's Nest Farm. The grasslands and their adjoining woods are a celebration of biodiversity, from the owls and warblers that haunt the woodland glades to the cowslips, harebells and wild thyme of the pastures and the rooks squabbling in the treetops.

In a hillside meadow there's a particularly rich community of wild flora. The rarest species is a low, broom-like plant with yellow flowers, Dyer's greenweed. Around it, among the waving grasses of summer, are others like lady's bedstraw, hawkbit and bird's-foot trefoil, while higher up on the escarpment the green sward is festooned with pyramid orchids and clustered bellflowers. Wild plants like this don't survive in spite of the farming. Nor do the myriad butterflies and insects that inhabit them. They are there because of the farming, or rather, the particular brand of farming practised by the Youngs.

Given the environmental and animal welfare benefits of the farming system, Kite's Nest Farm might seem the obvious candidate for any environmental payments going. Sadly this is not the case. This healthy, benign, wildlife-friendly form of agriculture doesn't tick the bureaucratic boxes of the official government scheme. While industrial farmers can pick up thousands of pounds by putting down small areas of land to wildlife habitat, farms like this one – where wildlife comes free as part of the system – are all too often excluded.

The Youngs are able to keep going in part because they're prepared to live frugally. Their love of the beautiful farm, its animals and wildlife are compensation enough for going without many of the trappings of modern, consumer life. Even so, they have substantial bills to pay to keep the farm running. It's only because they can sell direct to customers who value their beef that they're able to keep the business afloat.

When people buy at the little farm shop they're paying not just for the beef but for hawkbit and bellflower in the meadow and warblers and owls in the woods. They're also contributing to the contented, stress-free lives of the cattle grazing the rich pastures. All this plus some of the finest-tasting beef in the land seems bargain enough to the regulars who shop there.

If governments were serious about ending the steady loss of biodiversity in Britain, it's surely this kind of farming they'd support with state subsidies? Sadly they seem unwilling to confront the powerful agribusiness lobby, so the money gets spent on greening up industrial agriculture at the margins. This doesn't change the nature of the beast, which is basically hostile to wildlife and destructive of habitats.

But where the politicians fail consumer power can bring about change. The customers who regularly buy their beef at Kite's Nest Farm are voting for, and helping to create, a diverse and beautiful landscape, rich in wildlife. And whether they realise it or not, that same living landscape – with its fertile soils teeming with life – is putting extra nutrients into their diet. The farming systems that protect the life of the countryside are protecting the health of the people who live on it, too.

Around the country there are dozens, perhaps hundreds, of farms producing high-quality meat from traditional mixed pastures. The mass market food chain largely ignores them. But the signs are that there's going to be a great deal more of this wonderful meat around if only we'll take the trouble of seeking it out.

Ironically, it's the very scarcity of traditional, flower-rich grasslands that have brought about a revival in their products. Many of the surviving meadows and pastures are now designated as nature reserves or are protected as special sites. Conservationists have at last realised that the only way to keep them in good shape is to restore traditional grazing patterns using native breeds of cattle and sheep. As conservation bodies and wildlife groups set up these schemes, they look for ways of marketing the meat as a premium product. As a result there's a lot more healthy lamb and beef on the market, much of it selling locally.

Under one such scheme farmers in the Yorkshire Dales are selling the beef of hill breeds like the Belted Galloway that have been raised on the flower-rich pastures of "limestone country". Over centuries of traditional grazing these pastures have developed their own particular flora, dominated by blue moor grass and containing such species as rockrose, small scabious, bloody crane's bill and wild thyme. Under the scheme known as the Limestone Country Project, farmers are being helped to set up new herds of native cattle and sell the beef direct to consumers.

On the north-west coast of the Hebridean island of Islay, looking out directly on the wild north Atlantic, Eric and Sue Bignal have re-established traditional grazing on a rich mix of habitats that have been formed by centuries of grazing. They include areas of acid grassland, lime-loving grassland, dry heaths and marshes.

This rich mosaic of vegetation has given the island one of the richest and most diverse bird populations in the world, including ten protected species. The traditional grazing patterns have also created conditions needed by a wide range of invertebrates, especially butterflies. Among those that flourish on Islay are the threatened marsh fritillary, which breeds in damp acid grassland where the main food plant is devil's bit scabious.

With the decline of small farms and crofting, there was a risk that this rich mix of wildlife would be slowly eroded. But the Bignals have shown that by allowing native Highland cattle and hardy blackface sheep to range freely over this open, windswept landscape, it's possible to maintain the species diversity and so protect the wildlife.[5] The meat is marketed under the brand Highland Drovers, giving consumers a chance to share in the protection of this unique wildlife resource while enjoying foods of unique quality.

The open grasslands and marshes of Islay are typical of many areas across Europe that are rich in wildlife and which have been created by centuries of grazing by farm livestock. Living in lowland Britain it's easy to think that intensive industrial agriculture has damaged all our rural wildlife and that diverse habitats survive only in nature reserves. But in the wider world things are a little more complex.

While substantial areas of Europe have been impoverished by chemical agriculture, significant areas – perhaps as much as thirty million hectares in total – are still open land covered by natural vegetation. This is land managed by "extensive" grazing, – grazing with relatively low numbers of livestock. It's what the geographers call "extensive pastoralism".

These landscapes have survived destruction by the EU's common agricultural policy principally because they are in remote or mountainous areas where farming is difficult to intensify. In La Crau, an area of south-eastern France, sheep are moved from the local semi-natural grasslands to distant Alpine pastures for the summer. In the Carpathian Mountains of Romania and the Gredos of central Spain sheep, goats and cattle are also moved from lower ground to upland pastures in summer.

Because of the "high nature value" of these landscapes the EU Commission got together a group of specialists to look at how they could be better protected in the future. David McCracken from the Scottish Agricultural College, one of the UK members of the group, believes the chief threat to these "high nature value" grazing systems arises from a widespread misunderstanding of their importance to biodiversity. It's a misunderstanding shared by politicians, farmers, consumers, even ecologists and conservationists, he says.[6] He wants to see EU policymakers develop support schemes aimed specifically at regions of high nature value or at particular production systems. There's a special need for funding to protect "transhumance", the traditional practise of moving sheep, goats and cattle to distant grazings for parts of the year.

Whether the policymakers will be brave enough to take on the agri-business lobby is anyone's guess. What's certain is that we consumers can do a great deal to restore Britain's wildlife by choosing to eat pasture-fed foods.

Simply by asking for meat and dairy products that have been raised on grassland we're helping to increase biodiversity on these islands. Whether it's a joint of beef from a herd grazing a remote Scottish moorland or a species-rich stretch of English chalk downland, our spending at the check-out can put wildflowers, butterflies and birds back into the countryside. Even a glass of milk from cows on a hard-grazed pasture will have an environmental impact. It'll be helping raise the fertility of the soil, the subterranean wealth bank that powers life on the land.

Organic farms are known to be better for wildlife than conventional, chemical-dependent farms. In a five-year study across Britain, environmental scientists found that, compared with conventional farms, organic farms contained 85 per cent more plant species, one-third more bats, 17 per cent more spiders and 5 per cent more birds.[7]

The key feature that makes organic farms so good for wildlife is the mixed-farming principle with its short-term grass ley, the fertility-building heart of the entire system. While it would take many decades to rebuild the nation's wildlife by converting all Britain's farmland to organic methods, every farm in the country could introduce grass and grazing. The improvement in biodiversity would be immediate and spectacular.

On the south-east coast of the Isle of Wight, a world away from the windswept island of Islay, retired businessman Michael Poland has created a new grazing landscape that's both profitable for farming and rich in biodiversity. It includes unimproved chalk grassland and rough lowland grass, as well as some ancient woodlands.

Chalk grassland – the community of grasses and herbs that thrive in the alkaline conditions of soils overlying chalk – has become rare in Britain. So have the insects and other invertebrates that depend on this habitat. As we've seen, most have been destroyed by nitrate fertilizers and the intensification of agriculture.

But on Michael Poland's Wroxall Manor Farm near Ventnor, species-rich chalk grasslands flourish. Among a rich array of wild plants are a number of iconic species including bee orchids, early gentians and, in some fields, cowslips on a grand scale. Key to maintaining the grasslands in good shape is the farm's large herd of Highland cattle.

Highlands are ideal animals for maintaining species-rich grasslands. They are hardy grazers, thriving outdoors in all weathers and eating shrubby vegetation that most cattle wouldn't touch. They graze off the brambles and other shrubs that would otherwise shade out the nectar-rich flowers which support valuable butterfly species such as the Adonis Blue and the Chalkhill Blue.

In winter the cattle, in groups of about twenty animals, are put onto the species-rich downland to remove the summer growth and prepare a good, short turf to encourage herbs and wild flowers. In spring and summer the cattle are moved onto the lowlands where they graze the rough grassland and semi-improved grassland areas. This helps to spread wild flowers across the farm.

"The important thing is the beasts are free to range," says Michael. "You could call it grazing with a light touch. The animals decide where they want to go, so no pastures are over-grazed."

Wroxall Manor Farm is part of the Wight Conservation Estate, which manages over eight hundred hectares on the island. The whole thing is Michael's idea. Since setting up the project in the mid 1990s he has tried to combine profitable, low-input farming with the maintenance of rich biodiversity.

Some of the newer areas of chalk grassland are in fields that, not long ago, were growing heavily subsidised arable crops such as linseed. Now grassland dominates the landscape in this beautiful part of the Isle of Wight overlooking the Solent. Yet this traditional type of extensive farming is also profitable, thanks to good management and the power of grass.

The herd of Highlands is becoming increasingly well known. The estate has bred a number of champion bulls and cows, which helps to raise the value of breeding stock sold off to other farms. The superb beef produced on the herb-rich pastures is now highly sought after. All of which comes close to achieving Michael's aim of blending good conservation with commercial farming.

This estate, on the high chalk country of the Isle of Wight, and the windswept isle of Islay off the Scottish coast could become beacons for the evolution of a new landscape in Britain, - a post-peak oil landscape, high in biodiversity and producing healthy food. Except that it wouldn't be new.

This landscape of grass is older than the nation. What's new is the realisation that it meets our modern needs better than the landscape of industrial agriculture we have replaced it with.

It was Britain's great pastoral culture that made these islands so spectacularly beautiful. Grassland and grazing created William Blake's "green and pleasant land". They will do so again if we remain true to this wonderful cultural heritage.

9

Designs for a new country

From the genteel Hampshire village of Martin the chalk downs roll away southward like an ocean swell. Once they were covered in chalk grasslands and grazed by numerous flocks of downland sheep.

William Lawes, inspiration for Isaac Bawcombe in W. H. Hudson's classic book A Shepherd's Life, lies buried in the village churchyard.

Today the sheep and the shepherds have gone from the downs. So has the flower-filled grassland. Most of the fields are now sown with wheat and oilseeds, industrial crops for factory processing and global marketing.

For long-time resident Nick Snelgar this came as a great disappointment. Along with the other villagers, he was in the habit of driving ten miles or so to one of the local supermarkets for his food. When he got there it wasn't all that cheap and it wasn't particularly inspiring.

Why, he wondered, weren't some of the fields around the village growing fresh, wholesome food for the locals, just as they had done for centuries? Why were today's villagers having to buy foods they knew next to nothing about and which could have been sourced from anywhere? So he hatched a plan. What if the locals were to get together with one or two of the farmers to establish a truly local food supply, one that would produce to the highest standards at reasonable prices?

Filled with enthusiasm he approached all eight farmers in the parish. This was when he experienced his first setback. None of them were interested. Though they applauded his idealism, they thought his plan could never work. Like it or not, they were locked into the global grain system.

But having been gripped by an idea, Nick's not a person to let it go lightly. Undeterred, he pressed ahead with his plan. He got together a group of like-minded village residents and in true British tradition they formed a committee. He began searching for small parcels of land they could rent, while at the same time looking for people with horticultural and farming skills to work part-time on the project.

The outcome is a non-profit making co-operative called Future Farms.[1] It is now selling fresh, healthy foods to more than a hundred of Martin's one hundred and sixty four households. Every Saturday there's a market in the village hall, where seasonal vegetables go on sale alongside home-produced chicken, bacon and pork, all produced from animals on herb-rich pasture.

Though not formally designated "organic", this food is probably the healthiest you could buy. No chemical fertilizers or pesticides are used in its production. Soil fertility is maintained through the use of compost, clover-rich grass leys and pastured animals.

The pigs, mostly Wessex Saddlebacks, are raised and finished in outdoor arks set in species-rich grassland. The chickens, a slow-growing outdoor breed, are genuinely free-range. Housed in small huts on wooden sleds, they are regularly moved onto fresh pastures. Throughout the daylight hours they're out pecking at herbs and insects in the grass and hedges. Dressed for the oven they look lean and muscular; the sort of birds you don't see in supermarkets and which you know are going to taste superb.

The group's decision not to go for full organic status was carefully thought out, explains Nick. For one thing the formal conversion and designation process is expensive for small-scale operators like Future Farms. At the same time there's a suspicion that organic food has become an expensive niche market, not the sort of image the group want for their foods.

"We believe healthy food should be available to everyone, not just a well-off elite," says Nick. "We're careful to price our foods at about the level of the cheaper supermarkets. Yet ours are incomparably better. The vegetables are on sale within hours of coming out of the ground. Supermarket vegetables are often a week old by the time they go on the shelves.

"Our free-range chickens sell oven-ready at about £7.50 each. I've seen organic chickens on sale at the local farmers' market for £17. I believe ours are at least as good, probably better."

The next step is to add a small dairy unit based on pasture-fed

Red Poll cattle. This will supply dairy foods such as home-made cheeses and yogurt as well as fresh milk. The cows will spend much of the year on species-rich grassland. As we've seen, dairy foods produced this way are likely to be healthier than anything you'd find in a modern supermarket, organic or non-organic.

Through the co-op, they'll sell at prices most people can afford. What's more, the pricing system will be fully transparent. Full details of every cost element in the production of a food will be provided for customers. So they'll know that the prices are "real" and not based on modern marketing notions about what the consumer might be prepared to pay.

The ultimate aim is a traditional mixed farm, harnessing the productive power of grass leys to produce healthy foods which safeguard the environment. Nick intends to employ a young farming family full-time to run the enterprise, paying them a good salary to do the job. He's convinced that local, direct selling produces enough profit even with competitive pricing.

It's a marketing model he believes could be reproduced almost anywhere in Britain, including urban areas. His aim is to try out the scheme in a city, first recruiting a hundred or so families to set up their own co-op, then contracting farmers close to the city to produce high-quality food by traditional mixed farming methods. The scheme will guarantee good returns to farmers and healthy, nutrient-dense foods for members.

"This is about the nation's health," says Nick. "If we really care about it we need to be as devoted to our food supply as we are to the health service. Food is as important – perhaps more important – than medical services."

Future Farms is proving that the best-quality, healthiest foods need not be expensive or elitist. High prices have more to do with wasteful production methods and marketing structures designed to make profits for large companies.

Food produced by natural methods is invariably cheaper and healthier, particularly when based on the productivity of grassland. Future Farms is just one of hundreds of enterprises up and down the country which aim to harness the productive power of grass.

In the scale of operations it would be hard to find a greater contrast than Jody Scheckter's thousand-hectare project near Basingtoke. Step into the office reception area of his Hampshire farm and you'll see a couple of pictures that neatly sum up his philosophy. One of them shows a 1969 Ferrari racing car as driven by the man who went on to become world Formula One champion. On the opposite wall hangs a picture of a Hereford cow placidly chewing the cud on a lush, green pasture.

The Ferrari represents science, the finest technology, the modern world. The cow, from a famous English breed, is a product of an older cultural tradition; one based on knowledge of the seasons and the soil.

Jody Scheckter uses both at Laverstoke Park, Overton. When he took on the estate he decided that, for the sake of the family, he would produce the healthiest food possible, without compromise. Finding out exactly what constituted healthy food took him on a long journey of discovery. He talked to leading scientists and read the most up-to-date research reports.

His farm now makes use of an array of scientific gadgetry. There's a state-of-the-art abattoir, for instance. "What's the point in producing the best beef in the world if you're going to stress the animals by crowding them into a lorry and trucking them miles to slaughter?" he says.

Then there's the fully-equipped laboratory capable of measuring the mineral content and microbial life of soils and composts, as well as the mineral content of plant material. Hardly a facility you'd find on most farms.

Yet despite the high-tech gadgetry, the landscape Scheckter has created in pursuit of healthy food might have come straight from Thomas Hardy. The pastures are full of old grasses and wild herbs of the sort hardly seen on farms since the dawn of the chemical era. Walking through one of the Laverstoke Park fields I recognised some of them from my own little paddock of unsprayed grassland on Exmoor.

Among the grasses were such old farming stalwarts as cocksfoot, meadow fescue, timothy and rough stalked meadow grass. Among the flowers and herbs were chicory, kidney vetch, bird's-foot trefoil, fennel, salad burnet and ribwort plantain. There were also plenty of nitrogen-fixing clovers. Perennial ryegrass – favourite of agribusiness for its ability to thrive on chemical fertilizers – was nowhere to be seen.

These species weren't in the pastures by chance. They'd been sown as part of a chosen seeds mixture. When farm staff plant a new grass "ley" at Laverstoke Park they now include more than thirty species. Among them are deep rooting herbs like chicory which help get air and organic matter deep into the soil and, at the same time, bring up minerals. This means the animals grazing the pastures get plenty of essential trace elements in their rations.

In this essentially Victorian landscape livestock, too, are different from their modern equivalents. Having studied the kind of animals that produce the healthiest foods, Jody Scheckter has turned his back on modern breeds. He argues that, for the most part, they're the result of breeding programmes aimed at producing animals that will grow quickly on the minimum amount of food. This makes them more vulnerable to sickness and disease. As a consequence they're more reliant on antibiotics to keep them going.

What he's looking for are the older, native breeds of animals. They are slow-growing, hardy and resilient, he says. This means they are better suited to the outdoor life of an organic farm. They thrive on a natural diet of grasses and herbs, and convert more feed energy into meat.

Sometimes he's not even satisfied with the latest manifestations of traditional breeds. In the commercial world many have been "improved" by cross-breeding to make them more competitive with fast-growing modern breeds. In the process some of the beef quality has been lost.

To counter this development Scheckter "breeds back" to try and make his traditional herds more like the originals. For example, Laverstoke Park now has thirteen of only forty-five pure Native Angus cattle left in Britain.

The Aberdeen Angus is one of Scotland's most famous beef breeds, bred originally in Strathmore, between Angus and Perthshire. The small, hornless breed is hardy and docile. It became world renowned for the succulence and tenderness of its beef.

According to Scheckter, the modern Angus has been cross-bred for faster growth. So he has selected some of the few remaining examples of the pure native breed and these are being bred-back with other traditional types of Angus in an attempt to restore the quality beef of the original animal.

It's all part of the healthy-food-without-compromise philosophy that drives the farming revolution taking place in these Hampshire fields. As well as traditional Angus and Hereford cattle, there are British Saddleback and Middle White pigs; Hebridean, Lleyn and Polled Dorset sheep; Jersey cows; milking sheep and goats; and traditional breeds of poultry. There are also water buffalo, kept for their meat and creamy milk. Everything in this wonderful menagerie of food animals is rotated around the species-rich pastures.

Underpinning the whole diverse system are healthy, living soils. "Do you know a handful of soil contains more living things than there are people on earth?" he asked me as he sat across the desk outlining the farming system. Well no, I didn't, though I knew it was an awful lot.

With an in-house laboratory at Laverstoke Park, staff can keep track of a fair few of them. The microbes that matter are the ones that play a role in re-cycling nutrients, taking them from the dung produced by the daily parade of grazing animals and processing them into forms that can be used by the pasture grasses and herbs. The most important soil life-forms include bacteria, fungi, protozoa (single-celled organisms that feed on bacteria) and nematodes, a ubiquitous group made up of small worms.

Keeping them all healthy and active is a key part of managing an organic farm like this, one that's soon to adopt the more holistic approach of biodynamic agriculture. Jody Scheckter is one of the first farmers in Britain to make use of "compost teas". These are cold-water preparations made from compost. They contain nutrients and active micro-organisms, and can be applied directly to the soil or sprayed onto plants as a liquid feed.

In the soil these beneficial microbes boost the level of biological activity and form protective barriers around plant roots. On leaves they help protect the plant from attack by disease organisms.

It's all a far cry from the fields of regimented hybrid wheat crops – with their attendant boom sprayers – that cover much of lowland Britain. Yet I can't escape the feeling that it's the landscape of Laverstoke Park that will endure. It is, after all, a landscape that has served the country well for centuries. And as the twin pressures of climate change and food insecurity bear down ever more powerfully on the people of these islands, it's difficult to see how any other form of agriculture can thrive long term.

What Jody Scheckter has embarked upon, and in which he has invested a good deal of money, is a unique and important experiment. He started out by looking for the farming system that would produce the healthiest possible food. Having spent a lot of money setting it up, he is now concerned to find ways of making it pay.

But to the rest of us, what makes the experiment so interesting is that it's an attempt to devise a farming system that puts consumers in the driving seat. Ask anyone in the present food supply system "who drives it?" and they'll undoubtedly reply that it's the consumer. In theory it's the choices we all make in the supermarket which determine the foods that go on the shelves.

It's a delusion. No shopper decided that many of our staple foods should be produced from industrial grains rather than pastures. The crucial factor was that grains suited the industry from large farmers to traders to food manufacturers.

The most that can be said is that consumers by and large didn't dissent when their traditional foods were dumbed down. With their huge palette of colours and flavourings – plus some slick advertising – the food manufacturers somehow convinced us that what we wanted to buy was what they'd already decided to give us.

Jody Scheckter's project cuts through the marketing double-speak. It simply poses the question – how do you produce the healthiest food? This is surely the production model that's truly driven in the consumer interest? This is why the flower-filled pastures, the sturdy animals and the landscape of Laverstoke Park are such powerful indicators of how things ought to be, and how they may be before very much longer.

When you log onto the Laverstoke Park website and click on "human health", you're presented with a handy summary of the conclusions of American dentist Weston Price from his mammoth study of the diets of the world's healthiest peoples.[2] Price's principal conclusion was that people stay healthy when they eat what you might call the "naturally grown foods of the countryside". And they get sick when they eat industrial foods – processed products, refined carbohydrates such as sugar and white flour, and margarines.

If Price were around today it's likely that he'd add skimmed milk, low-fat dairy foods and vegetable oil spreads to his list of unhealthy foods. These are products of the food manufacturing industry. They're also the foods that today's healthy-eating campaigners promote at every opportunity. Can it be coincidence that so much official nutritional advice appears to favour the food industry?

For Jody Scheckter, as for Weston Price, the best foods come from plants and animals grown slowly on fertile, biologically-healthy soils. "Slow" is a key principle at Laverstoke Farm. Meat and dairy animals grow slowly on their diverse plant diets; pasture plants are given plenty of time to recover between grazings.

Slow could be interpreted as "natural" or "in nature's time". Over the medium and long-term it's almost always more efficient than industrial methods. And notwithstanding the huge cost of Jody Scheckter's ambitious experiment, nature's likely to prove cheaper in the long run; certainly if the external costs of industrial farming – pollution, environmental degradation, climate effects and ill-health – are added into the equation.

Two hundred miles or so to the west of Laverstoke Park, Ben Mead is on a similar journey of discovery. Ben's a farmer and cheese-maker. As well as running a herd of dairy cows, he and his wife Catherine, a marketing specialist, make the renowned Cornish Yarg cheese in a dairy at Ponsanooth near Truro.

Like the fields at Laverstoke, the pastures Ben's cows graze are filled with wild plants including bird's-foot trefoil, plantain, yarrow and chicory, as well as clover and a variety of different grasses. No nitrate fertilizer ever gets put on these pastures. Instead they're sprayed with compost teas supplying beneficial bacteria and fungi. The purpose is not so much to provide plant nutrients as to boost the biological activity of the soil, ensuring that the grasses and herbs are better nourished.

Ben's aim is to create a "super-turf", one so rich in minerals and vitamins that the cows in their turn will produce copious amounts of healthy, nutrient-rich milk, in dry seasons and in wet, all without the need for chemicals.

Ultimately the plan is to improve the tarnished image of milk, making it what it once was – a truly healthy food. Ben sums up his philosophy as one of "seeking nature's approval" for whatever he does to the land. He's convinced that natural processes are invariably the most productive, supplying better food in larger amounts.

He explains: "I've always been intrigued by stories of the early European settlers in North America. There was something in the land they inherited from the great prairie grasslands that enabled it to carry huge numbers of livestock, far more than our modern industrial agriculture can support.

"These are the conditions I'm trying to reproduce here in Cornwall. You could call it biological farming. It's a return to natural processes because our experience has shown them to be more efficient. And it's my belief the nutrient-dense foods they produce are healthier."

Ben currently runs a herd of 93 pasture-fed dairy cows on his farm at Pengreep. With Catherine, he diversified into cheese-making in 2001. The couple built a milk-processing plant which now operates in collaboration with the Lynher Dairies Cheese Company, makers of the famous Cornish Yarg cheese.[3] Ben's next project is to develop an unpasteurized cheese from the milk he produces on his flower-rich pastures.

If it tastes anything like the wonderful Comté cheese that comes from pastures like this in the French Jura, it should be a sure-fire winner. It's foods like this that will bring family dairy farms back to western Britain. In the Jura they're thriving.

The day I called at Pengreep the young replacement heifers were up to their bellies in blue-flowering chicory. This is the plant that Newman Turner, the 1950s pioneer of this kind of mixed-pasture dairy farming, praised above almost every other pasture species. He believed it supplied more minerals and trace elements, vitamins and plant hormones than pretty well any other plant.

Chicory's thick tap root can easily grow down three metres or more, searching for moisture in dry weather, and bringing up minerals to keep grazing animals healthy and fertile. Turner tells the story of the summer of drought in 1955, when most Somerset grass fields had been baked brown. His own herb-filled pastures stayed lush and green, principally because of the high proportion of chicory seeds that had gone into the original planting mixtures.

Looking at Ben Mead's replacement heifers in the bright July sunshine, I had no trouble accepting those early anecdotes of the wonders of chicory. The animals' coats gleamed and their eyes sparkled as they crowded around us with obvious curiosity. I didn't need Ben to tell me that the vet's a rare visitor on this farm.

Next we took a look at the milking cows. It was getting near lunch time and they'd all but grazed off the morning paddock. When we clambered off the quad bike they were already yelling to be allowed into the next paddock, with its tempting buffet of fresh green leaves and tall, stemmy grasses. To me these mature animals looked as healthy and athletic as the young stock, so different from the over-worked black-and-white cows I'd seen on my travels around Britain.

As he unhooked the electric fence, Ben pointed out a couple of elderly individuals still producing copious amounts of milk at twelve years of age. The scourges of modern dairy farming – infertility, lameness and udder infection – hardly register here. Fertility rates are extraordinary by dairy industry standards – more than 90 per cent conception within six weeks.

Ben told me of a recent visit from a research team based at Bristol veterinary school. They were travelling around West Country dairy farms looking at levels of lameness and its likely causes. At Pengreep they hit upon a problem. They couldn't find any lameness and they had no idea why not. It seemed to be extensive on pretty well every other farm they visited.

In Ben's view the reason is partly genetic. His cows aren't the usual high-yielding Holsteins. He has bred his own dairy animal - a three-way cross between the Friesian, Jersey and Ayrshire. An attractive dark brown in colour, these cows are long-living, fertile and great converters of grass into nutrient-rich milk. And, as the research vets discovered, they have very strong feet.

The other reason for the near-absence of lameness is, of course, the diet. For much of the year these cows eat a highly-varied diet: grasses and herbs, supplemented with dried seaweed and minerals, together with leaves and vegetation browsed from hedgerows and over-hanging trees. That this diet keeps them healthy and productive is beyond question. The jury is still out on whether the milk from these super-fit cows can do the same for human health and fertility. But I'd be willing to bet on it. One thing I am sure of – the milk tastes superb.

Ben's quest for higher quality foods began years earlier when he returned to the family farm after a career as a motor industry journalist. This was soon after the trauma of BSE in the cattle industry. He began to question the practice of producing milk with the aid of bought-in feeds especially whole cereal grains. Unless they're soaked or sprouted to neutralise the toxic phytic acid, cereal grains are damaging to ruminants – as they can be to human beings.

Ben took to reading the works of leading grassland scientists such as the French biochemist Andre Voisin. They led him to believe that pasture was both the most healthy and the most productive feed for livestock. Yet when he tried to produce large amounts milk from chemically-fertilized ryegrass monocultures he seemed destined to fail. That's when he made the decision to try biological farming – farming without chemicals.

In 2005 he won a Nuffield scholarship to look at grassland farming in New Zealand, Australia and the United States. There he found a growing interest in "nutrient-dense" foods – especially pasture-fed products – and the natural, biological systems that produced them. In New Zealand he met a biological dairy farmer whose soils had become so fertile he hadn't bought in any feeds, sprays or fertilizers for five years, yet he was making double the profit of most farms in the district on half the land area.

Ben has brought the techniques, and the philosophy behind them, to his farm in Cornwall. His instinct is to simplify the business of dairy farming, and he's convinced the only way to do this is to follow nature's model – putting diversity into his pastures. He suspects this will prove as important to human health as to the health of grazing animals.

In the beautiful Panteg Valley in west Wales, where Geoff Spawton and Annie May raise beef from pedigree Highland Cattle, diversity goes with the territory. It's what makes the meat taste as it does.

During the long, slow production process, which typically takes four years or more, the cattle graze on moorland grasses and marsh plants; on gorse, brambles and wild raspberry; and on the fine-leaved fescue grasses, the nettles, the ash and the sycamore of the lowland pastures and hedges.

In Geoff Spawton's view it's exactly this dietary variety which makes the finished beef taste so good. As far as he's concerned, a single-species pasture produces meat that is bland-tasting and boring. By contrast, the eclectic mix of herbs and grasses his cattle graze gives the beef a rich and complex taste. So when you buy it, not only are you getting a superb piece of meat, you have the satisfaction of knowing that you're aiding the environment and the health of the planet.

Geoff and Annie have been breeding Highland Cattle in Wales for more than twenty years. They are joint founders of the Highland Cattle Club of Wales. Though the breed is Scottish, they've found that this hardy and resourceful animal thrives on the wild and varied landscapes that surround them.

The couple began farming with ordinary commercial cattle. But when BSE started to take a hold on the national herd in the late 1980s, they made the decision to supply their family and their customers with beef they knew to be safe and fully traceable. That's what made them switch to pedigree Highlands.

With pedigree stock it's possible to chart each individual's family tree with pinpoint accuracy. So you know the animal's full history. The Highland seemed right for them because of it can eat almost any sort of vegetation and produce high quality, marbled beef with a superb taste. It also happens to be a very docile breed, which makes the management far easier

As well as beef, the couple produce lamb and mutton on their farm, Gilfachwen, at Cellan near Lampeter. The breed of sheep they use is the Welsh Mountain, the native of the area. Like their cattle, the sheep graze on gorse and heather moors, giving the meat both the arome and taste of the wild grasses and plants they were raised on.

All the meats from the farm have "terroir" – that sense of place which imbues a food with flavours reflecting the characteristics of the soil and the local environment. It's one of the benefits of foods from animals which are allowed to grow at their natural pace, on communities of native plants that are unique to their particular locations. It's what makes them "real" foods, as opposed to the manufactured products that fill most of our supermarket shelves.

Much of the meat from Gilfachwen is sold to local customers who come back time and time again. Supplies of beef, mutton and lamb are limited. Whenever animals are due be slaughtered, Geoff sends out a newsletter alerting the "regulars" whose details are kept on a mailing list. Deliveries are free within the local area.

It's a system of food production and marketing that gives customers an intimate and on-going link with their local landscape. This particular farm happens to serve a market town, Lampeter, and the rural areas around it. But there is no reason why this approach to food and its procurement couldn't work everywhere in Britain, even in the cities.

The survival of green belts provides a wonderful opportunity to ring our large conurbations with grass farms like Gilfachwen, producing meat, dairy foods and poultry for the people of the city.

Organic farmers Jon and Lynne Perkin produce healthy, pasture-fed meat on a farm in a beautiful wooded valley beside the River Lyne in Cumbria. It would be hard to imagine a better way of producing meat than the one they've chosen. Their thirty-five or so beef cows are traditional Blue Greys and Galloways, slow-maturing breeds, famed for the taste of their beef and their ability to thrive on grass and forage.[4]

The cows are crossed with another legendary breed, the Beef Shorthorn, to produce crossbreds that are raised for beef. They spend their lives grazing the flower-rich meadows along the river bank, with deep-rooting herbs to supply a range of minerals. When they're ready, they're sent the thirty miles or so to a family-run abattoir in Lockerbie for slaughter. After hanging, the meat is butchered in a small butchery on the farm.

This is beef of the highest quality, tender and delicious, and rich in polyunsaturated fats that are characteristic of the healthiest red meats. It's the kind of beef you'd expect to find in the food hall at Harrods. But the Perkins have found a way to sell it to their Cumbrian customers at a price you'd pay for everyday meat in the High Street.

It's called community supported agriculture. Around a hundred regular customers make a monthly payment by standing order, then order their meat when they choose. As well as beef there's lamb from the farm's flock of Scottish Blackface ewes, and pork from pigs cross-bred from Saddleback sows and a Tamworth boar. Jon delivers the meat by refrigerated van.

It's a system that's unlikely to make the two of them rich. But it provides a regular monthly income, which they're glad of. Combined with income from farm-gate sales and sales at local markets, it's enough to keep them farming the way they want to. It also allows them to bring up their children in an environment that would be hard to beat.

Whiteholme Farm, Roweltown, near Carlisle is not a place you're likely to stumble on by accident. You reach it down a long lane that winds its way through a tangled oakwood. On the day I called, the first green haze of spring had begun to settle over the twisted tree trunks.

In the warm, comfortable kitchen I talked to Lynne and Jon about farming and its future. To them organic farming is simply "common sense" farming – working with nature instead of in opposition. Before taking the tenancy of Whiteholme and the adjoining Low Luckens Farm, they worked as managers of an organic farm in Berkshire.

They watched their neighbour – a conventional farmer – spray his wheat crop no fewer than fourteen times. That's fourteen chemical sprays on a food crop destined to end up in supermarket bread or the buns supplied to a burger chain. Far from being "conventional", it is chemical farmers who are the odd ones out, says Jon. Chemical fertilizers became like a drug. Managing without them could be a challenge, but food was the better for it. So was the environment.

We took a walk around the farm. It was clearly not the easiest land to manage. This is a high rainfall area, and many of the fields are on heavy clay soils, a perfect scenario for waterlogging and poor drainage. Jon pointed out the current bane of his life – a mass of rushes invading a pasture field. Without chemicals they were hard to deal with.

But for every natural disadvantage there were a dozen compensations. Among them were a string of wildflower meadows, magnificent rambling hedgerows, and strips of ancient woodland bordering the river. Within the woodland were a number of protected wildlife sites harbouring rare mosses, lichens and ferns.

Next we walked around the traditional farm buildings and took a look at the livestock. In the dark byre a dozen or so Galloway cows gazed at us in curiosity as they chewed on their silage. The large Shorthorn stock bull, who had been lying quietly in the corner, got slowly to his feet and stared at us amiably. There was no anxiety, no stress. All seemed calm and unhurried.

If I hadn't been several hundred miles from home I'd have signed the standing order there and then. It seems many locals are of the same mind. Very few drop out of the scheme except when moving from the area.

The Perkins encourage visitors to the farm. They organise an annual barbecue and farm walk for customers. There's also an organic resource centre that hosts visits from hundreds of school children each year.

Community supported agriculture takes many forms. Jon and Lynne are happy with their own arrangement under which customers take on a commitment to make regular monthly payments. But the farm is run by the couple themselves. In other schemes customers get together to share in the day-to-day decision making.

Close to the sparkling waters of the Moray Firth in north-east Scotland there's a remarkable herd of dairy cows. There are twenty-four of them. They're not the familiar black-and-white Holsteins that currently produce most of Britain's milk. These are red-and-white Ayrshires, the native Scottish cows once famed the world over for the quality of their milk.

Unlike the over-worked beasts stocking today's intensive herds, these cows live to a great age. On the day I called the oldest was nineteen.

Most of their placid, measured days are spent on the fertile pasture which covers this little farm. It contains plenty of clover to harness the fertility-building microbes that enrich soils with nitrogen.

The milk produced on these fertile grasslands is turned into traditional cheese. Here at Wester Lawrenceton Farm they make a Scottish cheese of the type known as "dunlop", a product long associated with the Ayrshire breed. This particular one is called "Sweetmilk". It's based on the cheese made by Barbara Gilmour, a seventeenth-century Scottish exile, who returned from Ireland with the recipe.

The other cheese made on this small, east coast farm is a full-fat version of traditional crofter's cheese, usually made from skimmed milk because, in this moist coastal climate, it was found to keep better. The new full-fat version is called "Carola". It's made by a hybrid method that blends the practices of Scottish crofters with those of the makers of French "tomme" cheese.

The most remarkable feature of these Scottish cheeses is that they combine the taste and the health-giving properties of traditional "peasant" cheeses, like those produced on Alpine pastures in France and Switzerland. Like Alpine cheeses, they are made from the milk of cows grazing species-rich pastures, so they're high in minerals and fat-soluble vitamins. And because the milk is unpasteurised, their power to promote good health and vitality is undiminished.

In an age when most cows are managed intensively in ever larger herds – and the cheese-making process has become a factory operation – Pam and Nick Rodway have found a way of producing cheese of the highest quality. They've done it with the help of a group of friends and relatives who have become "cow-sharers" in the project to produce healthy, life-enhancing food.

When Pam and Nick started farming at Wester Lawrenceton, their aim was to produce organic eggs and goats' milk cheese. Though friends wanted them to keep dairy cows, they didn't have the capital to establish a new herd. So friends offered to finance the project by making long-term loans. Each contributed five hundred pounds – roughly the price of an Ayrshire cow at the time. In return the cow-sharers receive annual interest of eight per cent - paid in the form of cheese.

Through this novel partnership the sharers get health-giving cheeses at a price far lower than they'd pay in a specialist cheese shop. The arrangement also gives them an added extra – a commodity impossible to put a value on. It gives them an involvement in real farming, - a stake in the cultivation of land and the care of livestock.

The Rodways do all they can to encourage cow-sharers and their families onto the farm. Many come and lend a hand at busy times. Children are invited to share in the naming of animals. That's why there are cows called Rhubarb, Crumble, Custard, and Syllabub at Wester Lawrence.

At Christmas, sharers join in the custom of singing carols to the animals in their byres. Then on February 1, the feast day of St Bride, patron saint of dairy women, everyone joins in the special celebration for the healthy, natural foods of the countryside.

The feast day falls exactly forty days after Christmas, the day before Candlemas. Everyone gathers to walk the boundaries of the farm in a re-enactment of the Celtic custom of "encompassing", or blessing the land. A fire is lit to burn the Christmas greenery, the flame being later brought into the house. Celtic songs and blessings are sung, most taken from the ancient collection known as Carmina Gadelica.

Afterwards there's a feast to celebrate healthy local foods. The farm's cheese-makers bring in small, celebratory cheeses and decorative butter. To accompany them there's a traditional "bannock" – a round, unleavened loaf made from oatmeal, wheatmeal, a primitive form of barley and buttermilk.

It's a custom with echoes of the spring celebration in the Loetschental Valley in Switzerland. There candles are made from the season's first butter, and the whole community gathers in the village church to thank God for this nutritious and life-preserving food.

At Wester Lawrenceton Farm the Bride Day Feast is eagerly awaited, says Pam Rodway, especially by the children. "There's great excitement when the butter and bannocks are brought in. The children think of them as party food – they treat them almost with reverence.

"It comes from their close connection with the farm and with the animals. It springs from that same deep relationship indigenous peoples have with their livestock, peoples such as the Masai in Africa.

"Food is so much more than a material necessity to be obtained at the lowest possible cost. This is what our contemporary culture has turned it into. But food – the growing and raising of it, no less than the eating of it – can do so much to enrich our lives. It's a spiritual gift as well as a material one. It is the very essence of our well-being."

For Pam, the links between food and culture are important for a healthy society. She heads her local chapter, or convivia, of the Slow Food movement, which celebrates and tries to protect local foods. They're seen as the reflection of an area's biodiversity, culture, skills and tradition. One of the movement's main aims is to safeguard the future for small-scale farmers and food producers.

Back in Hampshire, dairy farmers James and Helen Hague have taken a more conventional approach to linking their local community to the foods of grassland. In 2005 they set up a small, pasture-based dairy herd on a farm rented from the county council at Lyde Green, Rotherwick.[5] The aim was to sell healthy, fresh milk direct to people's homes in the neighbouring villages.

The business has gone from strength to strength. Local residents tasting genuinely farm fresh milk for the first time can't get enough of the stuff. Children, particularly, love the creamy taste of milk from cows grazing on clover-rich grassland for much of the year. In less than three years, Daisy's Dairy milk was being delivered to fifteen-hundred homes in the Rotherwick area, securing a good income for the farm and supplying a healthy food to the community.

Now national winner of the UKTV Local Food Hero award, and with a clutch of business prizes under his belt, James has bigger ambitions. He'd like to see dairy farmers across Britain direct marketing farm fresh milk, just as they did in the 1930s. He believes the movement would transform the health of both the community and the countryside.

In his view it's a win-win situation. Consumers get a better-tasting, fresher pint for around the price of supermarket "commodity" milk. At the same time more of the consumer "spend" stays in the local economy, instead of going as dividends to big company shareholders. That's why James wants to see locally-produced, farm-fresh milk available across Britain.

"We have to act to make our farming systems more sustainable or it'll be too late," he says. "Most dairy farmers could do what we're doing at Lyde Green Farm. Many have the resources and facilities to do it, but choose not to. Yet our experience shows there are plenty of people who'd love this milk if only they had the opportunity to buy it."

James and Helen set up their own processing and bottling dairy using second-hand equipment costing £15,000. They're convinced it's the best investment they ever made. Their delivery staff take the milk round at night so customers will have it fresh on the doorstep in time for breakfast.

It means that today's milk is on the breakfast table tomorrow morning. No supermarket or big dairy, not even those running their own doorstep delivery rounds, can match this level of freshness. When you add in the fact that Daisy's Dairy milk is for much of the year from cows grazing clover-rich pastures, it's clear the quality would be hard to beat.

Industrial feeds like soya and maize have no place in the ration.

In winter the cows are fed on home-made silage from the same clover-rich pastures, supplemented with small amounts of a mix of wheat and rapeseed.

Across Britain innovative pasture farmers are helping to reshape the countryside, making it a healthier, more prosperous place. By buying the products of grassland we as consumers can play a key part in this revolution.

10

Revolution in the fields

In the early summer of 2008, two stories appeared in the British press with sinister implications for our food supply. Not that you'd have known it from the down-page treatment they were given. Neither got front page status. They didn't even make page leads.

Yet taken together they add up to a dire warning about the future of food, our health and the life and vitality of the countryside. It's clear that unless we as consumers and citizens take action quickly, we'll lose all control of the foods we eat and the price we're made to pay for them.

We'll also see the steady erosion of cherished landscapes together with a new threat to our wild plants and animals. William Blake's green and pleasant land could become a captive country, and the people who boldly threw off feudalism could become yoked to a new lord-of-the-manor – a corporate one.

The first news item sounded innocuous enough. It reported the passing of a new Farm Bill through the United States Congress, despite opposition from President George Bush. The new Act provided for more than $300 billion in public support for the American farm sector over the next five years.[1]

Though George Bush wanted reform of the subsidy system, his attempted veto was overridden. This meant that at a time of spiralling world prices and widespread hunger, US farmers would go on picking up subsidies at the expense of farmers in poor countries. And global corporations would go on collecting big profits.

Researchers at Tufts University found that industrial-scale animal factories – owned and controlled by a handful of large corporations – made $35 billion in indirect subsidies by being able to buy feed grains below the cost of production.

At the same time global agribusiness companies were making equally large profits from trading the subsidised grain around the world. Following deregulation of the grain market under an earlier Farm Bill, Cargill's profits leaped by almost 1000 per cent from $280 million in 1997-8 to $2.34 billion in 2006-7.[2] In April 2008, Cargill reported net earnings of $1.03 billion for the third quarter, up 86 per cent on the same period the previous year.

According to the Minneapolis-based Institute for Agriculture and Trade Policy, global food corporations saw their profits rise when farm prices collapsed following deregulation of the grain market. Now they were making even more money as food prices soared to crisis levels. Deregulation had effectively privatised market information, making it easier for big firms to manipulate prices.

The other portentous news item on the future of food highlighted a report from an Ottawa-based environmental action group know as ETC. In its report the group warned that giant seed and pesticide companies were busy filing hundreds of patents on genes that could help crop plants resist the affects of climate change.[3]

BASF, the world's biggest chemical company, and Monsanto, the world's biggest seed company – together with Bayer, Syngenta, Dupont and a number of biotech partners – had between them filed more than 500 patent documents around the world on so-called "climate ready" genes. These are genes that the companies are planning to market in crops genetically engineered to withstand such stresses as drought, heat, cold, floods and soil salinity.

According to the ETC Group, the "Gene Giants", as it calls them, are gearing up for a big PR offensive. As the world climate becomes more erratic and the food crisis deepens, biotech companies aim to re-brand themselves as climate saviours. They will push GM crops as a silver bullet solution to the challenge of climate change.

Together the two news items provide a chilling glimpse of the future of food production, or at least one possible scenario. First, the American Farm Bill shows that, even at a time of soaring commodity prices, western governments are determined to go on giving subsidies to their own farmers. And let's remember that the EU continues to support the farming sector too. This means that grains are sold around the world at below the cost of production, damaging farmers in poor countries and making it impossible for them to invest in their own agriculture.

Increasingly western grain surpluses are traded around the world by large companies who control the market and prices. It's hardly a rational way to feed a hungry world; more a recipe for shortages and price volatility, the very things we've started to see.

Into this flawed system come the biotech companies with their "climate ready" GM crops. Even assuming their technologies work, their intervention will lead to even greater corporate control over the world's food supply. Following a series of buy-ups and amalgamations, the world's seven largest seed corporations already account for over half of all commercial crop seeds, valued at $22.9 billion.

The ETC Group fears that the intervention of Monsanto and the rest will not only concentrate corporate power, it will drive up costs, inhibit independent research and further undermine the rights of farmers to save and exchange seeds. Far from securing our food supply at a time of dramatic changes to the climate, it will make things a great deal worse.

Small farmers in poor countries have done least to bring on climate change, yet they are among its first victims. To survive they need – not a handful of GM varieties that have to be bought each year from global biotech companies – but genetically diverse crops, from which they can choose those best adapted to local conditions. This is how small farmers have responded to climate change for thousands of years. Plant breeding can be an important part of this strategy. But patented techno-fixes that put farmers forever under the control of global corporations are the last thing they need.

The corporate grab of the world's food supply isn't restricted to developing countries. The big agribusiness and biotech companies have western agriculture in their sights too. Monsanto, Bayer,

Syngenta, Dow, BASF and DuPont all have research programmes aimed at developing GM crops that can withstand drought conditions.[4] The research is focussed on major crops, including maize, soyabeans and wheat, in temperate zones.

The strategy is clear. The gene companies wish to make us dependent on their unproven technologies for seeds and for our very survival. We are supposed to feel so threatened by the dangers of climate change that we'll back GM crops as our way out. It might be easier to accept the idea if many of the companies now offering the GM solution weren't the same ones who damaged our soils with their pesticides.

Right now the corporate view of the world's food supply and how to secure it seems to have been accepted root and branch by the policy-makers. There's only one answer and that's to hand over the problem to industry. Modern technology will save us from starvation. In reality, as we've seen, this approach is likely to make matters worse.

To the industrial mind the living world is a machine. When this mindset was applied to agriculture, it perceived a need to speed everything up. So it came up with a means of doing just that, – a chemical stimulant in the form of nitrate fertilizer. When nitrates led to an explosion of crop pests and diseases, the industrial mind came up with another instant remedy, – pesticides.

Together the nitrates and the pesticides have produced a whole new set of problems. Carbon is being driven from the soil and released into the atmosphere to hasten climate change. Topsoil, the only guarantee we have that our grand-children and their children will be able to feed themselves, is being eroded away or contaminated with salt.

So now the industrial mind is working on a new technical fix – GM crops. The only certainty about these is that they'll bring with them a new set of problems, possibly far worse than the ones we're grappling with at the moment.

There's another way of thinking about the land and how we use it. It's a way of thinking that's far older than the industrial mindset. It probably goes right back to the time of the first farmers. You could call it the "peasant" mindset, though I realise this word has taken on a whole new meaning.

One of the definitions of "peasant" in the Oxford Dictionary is "a lout or boorish person". Obviously I'm not using the word in that sense. Nor am I using it in quite the sense of the first definition: "a countryman or countrywoman". A true peasant is far more than this.

I prefer to think of a peasant as one who has a deep knowledge of the land, and of the animals and plants that live on it or in it. It's a knowledge passed on from generation to generation, based on observation and experience, but seldom the result of formal measurement. So it's discounted by scientists, and ridiculed by corporations who buy the science they want. But it's a knowledge that has much to offer as we face a food crisis of our own making.

While the industrial mind constantly seeks magic bullets to correct the health and environmental mistakes it has made, the peasant mind would take a very different approach. The peasant would say: Let's not exploit the land as if it were a gold mine or an oil well, forced to deliver up all its riches until it's exhausted. Instead let's manage it in a way that retains its wealth, its "capital", so we live off the interest before passing it on – with its productive powers intact – to our children and their children. When communities deal with the land in this way they find it feeds them very well. It could do the same for us today.

The peasant view of the land survived well into the 20th century. Right up until World War Two it was held by the small farmers of west Somerset, for example. They provided a secure and sustainable food supply to the local community. When they finished a beef animal on the steep, hill grazings and sent it to the butcher, the land it came from remained as fertile and productive as at the start of the process. It still held large amounts of soil carbon. It still absorbed rainfall and resisted erosion.

Milk from the dairy herds on the small, mixed farms was not only high in the vitamins and unsaturated fats, it came from pastures that were - at the same time - rebuilding reserves of fertility that would feed people next year and the year after. No oil-rich fertilizers were used to grow the stream of vegetables, soft fruits, poultry and eggs that came from those small farms. The foods came year after year, season after season; gifts of the sun and a fertile soil.

As recently as 1950, Newman Turner, author of Fertility Farming, showed how species-rich pastures with deep rooting herbs could provide a sustainable supply of nutrient-packed dairy foods without chemicals or fertilizers. What's more, they eradicated TB and a host of other diseases in cattle.

More than fifty years after its publication his book reads like a practical manual on how to guarantee a supply of healthy food at a time of climate change. In today's anxious times you'd expect governments to be pouring research funds into investigating systems like this. Instead they are ignored. It's as if British agriculture had no history.

In the US it has been left to a resourceful and determined individual, the Virginia farmer Joel Salatin, to prove the amazing productivity of grazing-based production systems. With Britain's fine tradition of producing wonderful foods from grass, it's galling to have to look to America for inspiration. But I know of no one on these shores who's turning out such a range and quantity of high quality foods using intelligent, rotational grazing.

There may be a handful of UK farms that are doing as well or better. It's just that I haven't found them yet. They certainly used to be around during my student days in north Wales.

Today we are told our food supply is better provided by the likes of Monsanto, Cargill, Syngenta, Dow, and the rest of them. As a result, Big Arable has taken over most of lowland Britain. Where grassland survives it is mostly plastered with nitrate fertilizer, breaking down the organic matter and damaging soil structure. Whenever there's a heavy rain storm, the lanes run brown, white or red as the soil washes away; the fertility of the land is borne off to the sea.

Industrial agribusiness appears to have plenty of answers to the problems of its own making. A characteristic of the industrial approach is that it must maintain a constant stream of technical "breakthroughs" and amazing new products to solve our most pressing problems. It cannot accept that for thousands of years communities have fed themselves – often very well – without the new technologies.

Therefore the "problem" of damaged soils and changing

climates will be solved by GM crops. The "problem" of expensive meat will be overcome by the cloning of animals. One of the great dreams of agribusiness executives is that one day the biotech companies will develop crop plants that are able to "fix" nitrogen in the soil in the same way as clovers.

Imagine that; wheat and maize plants that can create their own fertility from atmospheric nitrogen. What a wonderful example of corporations using their ingenuity for the betterment of humanity. People don't like chemical nitrate fertilizers. Fine, the corporate mind will come up with a solution. So an army of plant breeders are to be kept busy for decades trying to transfer genes from clover and other legumes into annual crops.

Humanity, of course, doesn't need them. Traditional mixed farmers developed a perfectly sound method of providing the benefits of nitrogen fixation to grain crops, one that has been tried and tested over the centuries. It's simply to grow a clover-rich pasture for two or three years between each "run" of cereal crops. The clover "ley" enriches the soil with mineralised nitrogen which the following cereal crops are then able to take up.

Mixed farmers also had a clever way of putting clover and its fertility-building capabilities in even closer contact with cereal crops. It was a technique still used in the 1960s.

The technique was called under-sowing. First you sowed a grass seed mixture containing clover. Then into this seedbed you drilled your cereal crop. The grass came up with its clover plants, and through it grew the cereal. As the clover plants "fixed" atmospheric nitrogen in their root nodules, the mineralised element was made available to the cereal crop by the action of soil microbes. The cereal plants were effectively fertilized by the pasture species growing around them. In the autumn the cereal was harvested leaving a ready-made pasture for grazing with cattle or sheep.

These solar-powered solutions to fertilizing crop plants are quietly forgotten by the farmland industrialisers. They are of no interest because they're free, tested and available to farmers everywhere. Clover seeds can't be patented, so agribusiness companies ignore them and search for high-tech and riskier alternatives they can sell, such as GM crops with the nitrogen-fixing capability of clover.

In the 1970s, a French farmer and ecologist called Marc Bonfils developed his own ingenious adaptation of the traditional under-sowing technique.[5] He was able to grow spectacular wheat crops without fertilizers or pesticides. To do so he used old-fashioned wheat varieties which he believed were stronger and more robust than the modern, short-strawed hybrids beloved by today's arable farmers.

But the real genius of his method was that he planted his wheat into a low-growing clover crop. Nourished by the fertility of the nitrogen-fixing clover, the wheat bushes grew tall and strong. When harvested the following summer they produced bigger grain yields than conventional crops even though they had received no fertilizers or chemical sprays. Once the crop was harvested, next year's crop could be planted straight into the clover ley, exploiting the free fertility direct from the sun. It was a truly sustainable system with a low carbon footprint.

Needless to say it has been effectively airbrushed from history. With industrial wheat production causing so much damage to the planet, the case for a full scientific investigation of the Bonfils system would seem unanswerable. But agribusiness companies aren't going to pay for it. It'll cost them their fertilizer and pesticide sales without giving them an alternative product to sell. Instead they pour billions of dollars into the search for GM crops they can patent.

One of the more ludicrous projects of industrial agriculture is an attempt to "perennialise" annual crop plants. The idea arose from comments made by American plant geneticist Wes Jackson.[6] Looking at the perennial grasses and flowers of the tall-grass prairies of Kansas, he was struck by their productivity year after year. They needed no chemical fertilizers, pesticides or weed-killers to thrive.

Jackson compared their productivity with the annual crop plants he saw growing nearby. These included maize, wheat, sorghum, sunflowers and soyabeans. The disadvantages of basing the world's agriculture on these crops was obvious. The annuals were shallow rooting and costly to grow. Wherever they were farmed there were problems with soil erosion, loss of fertility and contamination of watercourses with fertilizers and chemicals. These fields were also eerily quiet, Jackson noticed, being devoid of wildlife.

As argued in this book, a rational response to these observations would have been to produce our animal foods from grasslands, or, at least, as many of them as possible. But in a bizarre twist, hundreds of scientists around the world are now trying to breed hybrid plants that yield like annuals but in other ways behave like perennials.

The technical difficulties are immense and the scientists reckon it may take fifty years to accomplish. What's certain is that it will cost billions of dollars. But it'll be worth it, say the scientists, because in the end it will mean fewer pesticides, greater biodiversity and a healthier environment.

No one seems to have told them that these benefits are available now, for free. The amazing new crop is called grass. Most of today's annual crops are fed to animals. Why not put the animals back on pastures and stop damaging our environment with fertilizers and pesticides? And for crops intended for human consumption such as bread wheat, why not grow them as part of mixed farming rotation and get the fertility-building benefits of grassland that way?

The principal aim of industrial agriculture is to develop a technology that can be applied virtually anywhere in the world. With Big Arable it has come pretty close to achieving its goal. Grain crops such as rice, maize and wheat are grown as monocultures across millions of hectares of farmland. The same hybrid strains are used everywhere so there's little genetic diversity. This makes them far more vulnerable to catastrophic collapse than more diverse ecosystems like species-rich grasslands.

Traditional farming adapts to local conditions. Family farmers have an intimate knowledge of their soils, the topography and the climate. They adapt their farming methods and cropping patterns to suit the local conditions. Hedges and field patterns, for instance, are arranged to minimise the risk of soil erosion. In traditional communities the loss of topsoil could well mean hunger.

The global strategy of industrial agriculture is to overwhelm such stable communities with Big Money and Big Technology. So the standard arable blueprint is rolled out across the countryside without regard to local conditions. The very word "local" is an anathema to agribusiness companies. As a result large-scale damage is done to the world's capacity to grow food.

If almost half Britain's soils are now so low in organic matter they are at risk of erosion, the world must be in serious trouble. Compared with many countries Britain has soils that are relatively stable. That they, too, are in a dire state is an indication of the threat now facing the world.

It's a threat acknowledged in a 2008 report from the World Bank and most UN agencies.[7] Based on the work of more than four hundred scientists, it concludes that the present system of food production – and the way food is traded – has led to an unequal distribution of benefits and to serious ecological damage. It is also contributing to climate change.

The report's authors reject GM crops as having any significant part to play in ending world hunger. They also criticise the growing of biofuel crops for cars, arguing that it is likely to increase worldwide malnutrition. What they want to see is more research targeted, not just at increasing crop yields, but at protecting soils, water and forests. "We urgently need sustainable ways to produce food," says Professor Robert Watson, director of multi-disciplinary group which produced the report.

At its launch a group of eight international environmental and consumer organisations commented: "This is a sobering account of the failure of industrial farming. Small-scale farmers using ecological methods provide the way forward to avert the food crisis and meet the needs of communities."

But industrial farming and Big Arable in particular are not about feeding people or meeting the needs of communities. Their main purpose is to concentrate wealth – the wealth of the land – into fewer and fewer hands; to enrich a handful of people at the expense of almost everyone else.

The American evolutionary biologist Jared Diamond investigates the process in his best-selling book, Guns, Germs, and Steel.[8] He describes how crop growing leads to centralised bureaucracies, military power and an oligarchy of wealth. Its main currency is grain. Power structures amass grain because its concentrated nutrients are easily stored, transported and traded. It provides security against hunger. Grain acts as a source of power.

In the past, societies like the ancient Egyptians, the Romans and the Mayans used grain to gain political power and domination. In recent times the United States and Europe have used it in much the same way, allowing large corporations to become post-colonial invaders.

Vandana Shiva has seen the tragedy unfold in her native India. Industrial agriculture, she says, wages economic warfare against the poor. Hunger in the developing world has grown in direct proportion to the spread of industrial agriculture and the globalisation of trade in staple foods.

"Industrial agriculture is an efficient system for robbing farmers of wealth and pushing them into debt and dispossession. The costly seeds, chemicals and machinery that replaced the farm's internal resources were originally supported through subsidies. Today they are obtained by borrowing from the same agents who sell the pesticides and seeds.

"A new phenomenon of corporate feudalism is emerging, as global seed and agrochemical corporations combine with the local feudal power of landlords and moneylenders to trap peasants into unpayable debt. More than twenty thousand Indian peasants have committed suicide since the seed and agriculture sector was opened up to global corporations. The worst suicides have occurred in Warangal in Andhra Pradesh.

"While the rhetoric of the Green Revolution and genetic engineering is the removal of hunger, the reality is that high-cost, high external input agriculture creates hunger by leaving nothing in rural households. Peasants must sell all they produce in order to pay back debts. This is why the producers of food are going hungry themselves."[9]

In Britain, as in other western countries, a similar process has taken place. Fortunately it hasn't resulted in mass starvation, and farmer suicides have been rare. But here, too, tens of thousands of small mixed farms have been forced out of business by the advance of Big Arable, backed by generous subsidies from taxpayers.

Apologists for industrial agriculture claim they were unproductive and inefficient. The opposite is true. Small mixed farms produce more food per hectare than large intensive farms. And because they are less reliant on oil, they are more efficient and sustainable.

The question we all face is not how the world will be fed, but who will control the land and, with it, the wealth of the land. If we want centralised control, large-scale production according to a standard "blueprint" that's applied to all the world's cropland, then we're pretty much on course. But if we believe countries should be largely responsible for producing their own food by rewarding their own farmers and using fully their own resources, then we're going to have to make changes. And in Britain that will mean restoring grassland to the heart of our food production.

Grass farming is our best chance – perhaps our only chance – of bringing food production back home. Meat and dairy products from pasture-fed animals are the only genuinely "local" animal foods you'll find. A shop may claim that intensively-reared chicken is local. But if it's out of a controlled-environment broiler shed, and it's been fed on cereals shipped in from Ohio or Ukraine, how is that chicken in any meaningful sense local?

By contrast, livestock raised on a local pasture are grown on the fertility of that place. It is the result of sunlight on a particular community of plants; of the biology of a particular soil; of the grazing animal's interaction with a unique set of plants and animals. As we've seen, it gives foods what the French call terroir, the sense of place, the sum of all the environmental influences on their production.

Sceptics may worry that grass farming won't produce enough to feed us. The opposite is true. Britain has twice the area under pasture than it has under cultivation for crops. Sadly this great resource has been underused for decades, perhaps centuries. With proper management it could become a huge and sustainable source of food.

It would also be a truly secure food supply. As we've seen, grain is too easily shipped to wherever the price is highest. Grain grown in Britain can't be held here, at least, not without government restrictions that would be unthinkable in a free trading world. And while most of our meat and dairy products are produced from grain, by exporting it we export our food supply as well.

Grasslands can't be shipped abroad. They'll go on clothing the hills, valleys and fields of Britain just as they've done throughout history. That's why the foods they produce represent a truly secure supply. No matter what happens to global markets, the price of oil, the price of fertilizer or to a large extent the weather, grasslands will go on producing foods of the healthy variety. What's more, with the right management they'll retain and build the fertility of the soil so that future generations of Britons will enjoy a secure food supply as well.

In the United States many farmers now recognise the potential of pasture farming. Appalled at the destruction of farming communities and biodiversity by industrial grain production, they see pasture farming as the catalyst for a real rural renaissance.

Ohio farmer and writer Gene Logsdon, himself a convert to pasture farming, describes it as the flowering of an "old-new agrarian way" of producing food. It means relying on grazing animals to provide meat, milk, eggs, dairy products, wool and hundreds of other animal products at a fraction of the cost of producing them with current factory technology.

"Pasture farming is the first alternative to high-tech agriculture that has both short-term and long-term profit on its side," Logsdon says. He is a passionate exponent of what he calls "managed intensive grazing" – the moving of grazing animals around a succession of grass paddocks. As a producer of low-cost, healthy food, he's convinced it beats grain production hands-down.

"Once the fields of grasses and clovers are established, spring work amounts to turning the animals onto pasture paddocks in rotation and watching them eat," he says. "Rains don't hamper soil cultivation because there is no soil cultivation. There is no erosion. There are no costly cultivation tools. Hailstones won't hurt the grass. Even flooding only harms it temporarily.

"The animals harvest the pasture crops, control most weeds by eating them, and spread their manure for fertilizer, all without labour, fuel or machinery expense. The amount of fertilizer and herbicides necessary to keep the pasture productive is minimal, and sometimes not needed at all. The farmer mends fences and makes hay.

"If he gets good at grass farming and uses all the pasture plants available, he'll have to make only a minimal amount of hay, just enough to supplement winter grazing. When he gets really good at grass management, the animals can pasture all year round except after heavy snows or, on some soils, for a short time during spring thaw.

"I don't think you have to be a genius to figure out which farming method is more economical – as well as ecologically sane."

In the spring of 2006 it began to look as if industrial farming would collapse under the weight of its own waste and inefficiency. The price of feed wheat had slumped so low that arable farmers were finding it hard to pay for all the fertilizers and pesticides they needed to keep the system going.

Things were no better in the livestock sector. Beef and lamb prices were low, and the milk industry was in such a mess that the Womens' Institute was obliged to run a campaign to save dairy farmers.

This can't go on much longer, I thought. Any time now livestock farmers are going to realise there's no future in this oil-guzzling system of production. They'll rediscover grass and the benefits of solar-powered farming.

It seemed Big Arable would have to change, too. It was only the EU subsidies that were keeping the system going. Sooner or later some hard-pressed farmer was going to try cutting his crippling fertilizer bill by sowing a few fields with clover-rich grassland in order to put the fertility back. Before you knew it they'd all be back into mixed farming, with beef and sheep, grass leys and rotations. And next time the pesticide rep called he'd get a chillier reception.

If you talk to arable farmers they'll tell you this can never happen. On Britain's great grain prairies there's no going back to livestock, they'll tell you. "We haven't got the staff." "The hedges have gone." "No one wants to do that sort of work any more".

I can well understand why a farmer who has been growing crops for twenty years might not relish the prospect of looking after animals once more. But there are plenty of ambitious young stock-keepers around just longing to get into beef and sheep rearing. It's easy enough to set up farm business tenancies or share farming agreements. With a few rolls of electric fencing they'd turn a grain desert into a fertile mixed farm in no time at all. Furthermore, everyone would benefit – especially the customers who eat the food.

In the event Big Arable didn't collapse – at least it hasn't done yet. Out of the blue the world food crisis came riding to the rescue, or perhaps more accurately, came along to tighten the shackles. The world price of wheat doubled in just a few months, and for the first time in years farmers felt they had something to celebrate. Sales of new tractors boomed and the price of land went steeply upward.

There are a number of ironies about the sudden escalation in the grain price and the salvation of industrial farming. One of the causes of rising prices was an increase in demand from China. While commentators have plenty to say about China's economic miracle and the desire of the middle class to spend some of their new wealth on meat – grain-fed, of course, - there has been little about the degradation of the country's own farmland by industrial agriculture.

China is the world's biggest producer and consumer of chemical fertilizers, and the second biggest consumer of pesticides. This is one of the reasons why 19 per cent of its soils have been seriously damaged by erosion, and why the country loses five billion tonnes of soil a year.[10] Damage is particularly severe on the once-fertile Loess Plateau of which 70 per cent is now eroded. Everywhere fertility and soil quality have been reduced by long-term use of fertilizers and pesticides.

The country's once productive grasslands have also been damaged by bad management. China is second only to Australia in the extent of its natural grasslands, which cover 40 per cent of the land area. Over-grazing has contributed to the degradation of 90 per cent of this great resource, so that grass production per hectare has fallen by 40 per cent since the 1950s.

In affect, industrial farming has destroyed a significant part of China's capacity to feed itself. And the country's response – buying food on world markets – is now causing the price rises which perpetuate this damaging form of food production in the west.

Then there's the question of biofuels. America and Europe's decision to bring in biofuel quotas will do little to counter climate change, but it's already given an enormous boost to industrial grain farmers. The quotas are, in reality, a new form of subsidy to Big Arable, the enterprise that has been most adept at extracting subsidies from governments.

For half a century, it has been subsidies to industrial farmers that have driven carbon out of soils and poured carbon dioxide into the atmosphere to hasten climate change. By what twisted logic were farmers able to persuade governments that shoving more fertilizer and pesticides onto grain crops would be good for the planet? As a lobby group they've been brilliantly successful.

As it happens, one sort of farm subsidy might bring real public benefits. As a general principle I'm not much in favour of giving farmers hand-outs from the taxpayer. However, there's one subsidy whose time has surely come. Why not offer farmers a cash payment based on the level of organic matter in their soils? It would be straight-forward enough to measure. Organic matter levels change slowly, so you'd only need to test soils every few years or so. Compared with the kind of bureaucracy used to dispense current subsidies under the so-called single farm payment, it would be simplicity itself.

A soil carbon subsidy would transform farming and change the world. For the first time it would give farmers an incentive to put carbon back into the soil. Not only would this be an enormous step in the fight against climate change, it is precisely the right prescription for improving the quality of our food.

Since one of the most effective ways of lifting soil carbon is to graze or otherwise harvest grassland, the measure would be certain to boost both the area under grass and the efficiency with which it is used. Gene Logsdon's system of "managed intensive grazing" would do it. We'd have a secure source of healthy, nutrient-rich, pasture-fed foods direct from our own countryside. At the same time our farmland could at last start to make an important impact in the battle against climate change.

Grassland, the crop that has contributed so much to the wealth of Britain – and to the beauty of its countryside – has been neglected since the onset of the oil age. It's now time to revive it. The country needs to genuinely "green up" its food production through the use of grass, that great, natural solar energy collector.

Despite the logic, there's no guarantee that the EU, the US government or any other state institution will introduce a soil carbon subsidy in the foreseeable future. Yet the greening of farming is a change that can't wait. If it is going to happen it will need us – as consumers and citizens – to reclaim our agriculture from the corporations while we still can. After all it doesn't belong to them. Nor, for that matter, does it belong to the government, the Crown, the National Farmers' Union, or even farmers. It belongs to us, the people of these islands. So if the policy-makers won't run it for the benefit of all of us, it's about time we forced their hand.

If we're going to eat meat and dairy foods, let's do our utmost to ensure they are from animals raised on grass. Look for foods like this in farm shops, farmers' markets and wholefood stores. Try good High Street butchers and delis. And, of course, check out the internet. Last time I Googled "grass fed beef" I turned up about ten thousand pages.

Many of them covered the latest science on pasture feeding and its effects on omega-3 and CLA in foods. There were plenty of sites offering grass-fed beef for home delivery. One of the best sites is a resource called Seeds of Health, which carries articles on the health benefits of grass-fed animal foods together with a list of suppliers.

Then there are the supermarkets. If enough of us start asking for grass-fed foods in our local superstore, it surely won't be long before the shelves and chill cabinets are full of them.

It's rather fashionable to attack supermarkets these days, particularly over their food policies. But the industrial farming lobby is strong, counting among its supporters large farmers, academics and policy-makers, as well as some of the most powerful industrial corporations on the planet. Consumer power - acting through supermarkets – could take them on and bring about change.

We need to make clear that eggs from pastured hens aren't enough. We need our beef, our lamb, our milk and dairy products to come from pastures, too. And while we're at it, pastured poultry and pastured pork ought to become the norm rather than the exception.

Given consumer demand, they'll quickly become mainstream items, and the grip of industrial agriculture on the wonderful British countryside will be loosened. We'll bring our foods and our farming back home at last.

I used to think the organic movement might bring about the change we need. I'm less optimistic now. Despite its new strength and influence, it will be decades before it feeds more than a small percentage of the population.

I remember being hugely inspired by some the movement's

pioneers, especially Albert Howard, the scientist turned food campaigner. Howard and his colleagues took the fight against the chemical-industry's take over of British farming as far as the House of Lords.

Today's organic movement seems to have lost heart for the battle. Its products sit on supermarket shelves, an expensive and profitable "brand" accounting for less than 2 per cent of the nation's food. Organic foods allow politicians to evade their responsibilities for ensuring stable and wholesome food supplies with the claim that consumers have the choice.

Healthy food is made a niche market and opposition to the deluge of second rate foods is blunted. Industrial agriculture is free to continue producing and selling its flawed products to the vast majority of the public.

Whether or not a farmer uses a small amount of nitrate fertilizer is of little consequence. By the simple act of taking food animals off their grain-based diets and putting them back on grassland, we would produce a huge improvement in the quality of the nation's food, one that would take the organic movement decades at the present rates of progress.

For all of us on these islands, the foods of grassland are our heritage. The landscapes created by their culture have been celebrated by our finest artists, musicians and writers. And the wealth they created put Britain on the road to greatness long before the Industrial Revolution.

In addition to producing healthy foods, we now need our grasslands to save our environment and our planet. Unlike the pedlars of farm chemicals and GM crops, they won't let us down.

Where to buy grass fed foods

The following suppliers are, to the best of our knowledge, producing foods from animals raised principally on grass. We don't claim this to be a comprehensive list. Sadly there are few financial rewards for producers who raise animals on pasture, so most fail to mention it in their promotional material. But there are undoubtedly many food producers – both organic and non-organic – who manage their farms sustainably by making good use of clover-rich and mixed-species grassland. They choose to do so because they have found it a cost-effective way to farm and because they want to safeguard the environment and, ultimately, our planet. By seeking out their produce we not only provide healthy food for ourselves and our families, we also help ensure there'll be more of it around in the future.

In drawing up this supplier list we've done our best to find producers who feed some or all of their livestock on pasture as a significant part of their diet. Many suppliers run a number of different animal enterprises on their farms. They've found this diversity of species to be highly productive, maintaining a good output while boosting the fertility of their land. To help you in your search we have used species icons to indicate which animals are grass-fed. Where seasonality is likely to influence the diet or the availability of their products we have indicated this with the following icon ✪.

We hope that in this book we've given you the information you need to seek out and find some of the healthiest foods going, while at the same time helping to save the planet. Our wonderful pastures are the best assurance we have of a secure, sustainable food supply now and in the future. By asking a few simple questions about the food you buy you can ensure the survival of this vital national resource. We wish you good fortune in your quest for real, grass-fed food.

Graham Harvey

NORTH

Blagdon Farm Shop
Unit 16-18, Milkhope Centre, Berwick Hill Road, Seaton Burn,
Newcastle upon Tyne, Northumberland, NE13 6DA
01670 789924
enquiries@theblagdonfarmshop.co.uk
www.theblagdonfarmshop.co.uk
🐄🐏🦃🐖🛒

Country Cuts Organic Meats
Bridge End Farm, Santon Bridge, Holmrook, Cumbria, CA19 1UY
01946 726256
www.country-cuts.co.uk
🐄🐏🦃🐖✉

Farmhouse Direct
Long Ghyll Farms, Brock Close, Bleasdale, Preston, PR3 1UZ
01995 61799
orders@farmhousedirect.com
www.farmhousedirect.com
🐄🐏🦃🦃✉

Farmhouse Direct
Long Ghyll Farms, Bleasdale Lane, Bleasdale, Preston, Lancashire,
PR3 1UZ
01995 61799
www.farmhousedirect.com
🐄🐏🦃🦃✉

Holly Tree Farm Shop
Chester Road, Tabley, Knutsford, Cheshire, WA16 0EU
01565 651835

Yew Tree Farm
Rosthwaite, Borrowdale, Keswick, Cumbria, CA12 5XB
01768 777675
www.yew-tree-farm.co.uk

Northumbrian Quality Meats

Monkridge Hill Farm, West Woodburn, Hexham, Northumberland, NE48 2TU
01434 270184
enqs@northumbrian-organic-meat.co.uk
www.northumbrian-organic-meat.co.uk

George Payne

27 Princes Road, Brunton Park, Gosforth, Newcastle-Upon-Tyne, NE3 5TT
01912 362992
www.georgepayne.co.uk

Keith Siddorn

Meadow Bank Farm, Broxton, Cheshire, CH3 9JS
01829 782117
keithsiddorn@fsnet.co.uk

MIDLANDS

Berkswell Traditional Farmstead Meats

Larges Farm, Back Lane, Meriden, Coventry, Solihull, CV7 7LD
01676 522409
www.farmsteadmeats.co.uk

Brocklebys Farm Shop

Melton Road, Asfordby Hill, Melton Mowbray, Leicestershire, LE14 3QU
01664 813200
order@brocklebys.co.uk
www.brocklebys.co.uk

Chantry Farm

Kings Newton Lane, Melbourne, Derby, Derbyshire, DE73 8DD
01332 865698
sales@chantryfarm.com
www.chantryfarm.com

Fordhall Organic Farm

Fordhall Organic Farm, Tern Hill Road, Market Drayton, Shropshire,
TF9 3PS
01630 638696
info@fordhallfarm.com
www.fordhallorganicfarm.co.uk

Goodman's Geese

Home Farm Lane, Great Witley, Worcester, Worcestershire, WR6 6JJ
01299 896272
sales@goodmansgeese.co.uk
www.goodmansgeese.co.uk

Happy Meats

Bank House Farm,
Stanford Bridge, Worcester, Worcestershire, WR6 6RU
01886 812485
Info@happymeats.co.uk
www.happymeats.co.uk

Llandinabo Farm Shop

21 The Homend, Ledbury, County of Herefordshire, HR8 1BN
01531 632744
mail@rarebreedsbutcher.com
www.llandinabofarmshop.co.uk

The Loop Farm

Cholmondeley Castle Farm Shop, Cholmondeley, Malpas, Cheshire,
SY14 8AQ
01691 624858
info@localproduce.org.uk
www.localproduce.org.uk

SOUTH EAST

Bank Farm
Bank Farm Produce ltd, Bank Road, Aldington, Ashford, Kent,
TN25 7YF
0800 5874999

Dove's
71 Northcote Road, London, SW11 6PJ
02072 235191
doveandson@aol.com

Lee House Farm
Lee House Farm, Plaistow, Billingshurst, Surrey, RH14 0PB
01403 753311
info@leehousefarm.co.uk
www.leehousefarm.co.uk
🐄🐖🐑🐷🥚✉🛒

Longwood Farm
Longwood Farm, Icklingham Road, Tuddenham, Bury St. Edmunds,
Suffolk, IP28 6TB
01638 717120
sales@longwoodfarm.co.uk
www.longwoodfarm.co.uk
🐄🐖🐓🐷✉🛒

Sussexway Meat
Ray Lodge Farm, Lingfield, RH7 6JH
07976 536848
david@sussexwaymeat.com
www.sussexwaymeat.com
🐄🐖🐑🥓✉🛒

SOUTH

Beacon Hill Farm
Bosbury, Ledbury, County of Herefordshire, HR8 1JY
01531 640275
beaconicecream@aol.com
www.beaconicecream.com

Blackburne & Haynes
Meadow Cottage Farm, Churt Road, Headley, Bordon, Hampshire, GU35 8SS
01428 712155

Dairy Barn Farm Shop
North Houghton, Stockbridge, Hampshire, SO20 6LF
01264 811405
dairybarnshop@aol.com
www.dairybarn.co.uk

Holly Bush Farm
Hollybush Lane, Eversley, Hook, Hampshire, RG27 0NH
01189 328816
www.hollybushfarm.com

Laverstoke Park Butcher's Shop
Southley Farm, Overton, Basingstoke, Hampshire, RG25 3DR
01256 771571
www.laverstokeparkbutchersshop.co.uk

Park Farm Shop
Near Hatchgate Pub, Heckfield, Hook, Hampshire, RG27 0LD
01189 326650
lyndsey@pfo-shop.co.uk
www.pfo-shop.co.uk

Sheepdrove Organic Farm
Warren Farm Office, Sheepdrove, Lambourne, Berkshire, RG17 7UU
01488 71659
andy_nash@sheepdrove.com
www.sheepdrove.com

Whitfield Farm Organics
Whitefiled Farm, Falfields, Wotten-Under-Edge, Goucester, GL12 8DR
01458 261010
jfb@whitfieldfarmorganics.co.uk

SOUTH WEST

Barrow Boar
Fosters Farm, South Barrow, Yeovil, Somerset, BA22 7LN
01963 440315
sales@barrowboar.co.uk
www.barrowboar.co.uk

Broadacre Farm
Broadacre Farm, Henly, Langport, Somerset, TA10 9 AY
01458 251883
enquiries@broadacrefarmshop.co.uk
www.broadacrefarmshop.co.uk

Brown Cow Organics
Perridge Farm, Pilton, Shepton Mallet, Somerset, BA4 4EW
01749 890298
enquiries@BrownCowOrganics.co.uk
www.browncoworganics.co.uk

Exmoor Organic Farmers
Hindon Organic Farm, Exford, Simonsbath, Minehead,
Somerset, TA24 7JY
01643 705244
info@hindonfarm.co.uk
www.exmoororganicmeat.co.uk

Fusland Farm
Fusland Farm, Moorlinch, Bridgwater, Somerset, TA7 9B2
01278 722386,
Stuart@norton8.orangegome.co.uk

Heritage Prime
Heritage Prime, Litton Cheney, Dorchester, Dorset, DT2 9AD
01308 482688
HeritagePrime@aol.com
www.heritageprime.co.uk

Higher Hacknell Farm
Higher Hacknell Farm, Burrington, Umberleigh, Devon, EX37 9LX
01769 560909
info@higherhacknell.co.uk
www.higherhacknell.co.uk

Owls Barn
Owls Barn, Derritt Lane, Sopley, Christchurch, Dorset, BH23 7AZ
01425 672239
shop@owlsbarn.com
www.owlsbarn.com

Pampered Pigs
Rye Hill Farmhouse, Rye Hill, Bere Regis, Wareham, Dorset, BH20 7LP
01929 472327
www.organic-pork.co.uk

Riverford Farmshop
Churchtown Farm, Lanteglos, Fowey, Cornwall and Isles of Scilly,
PL23 1NH
01726 870375
www.riverfordfarmshop.com

Cusgarne Wollas
Cusgarne Wollas, Cusgarne, Truro, Cornwall and Isles of Scilly,
TR4 8RL
01872 865922
organicbox@btconnect.com
www.cusgarne.org

Shoulders Farm
Shapwick Road, Westhay, Glastonbury, Somerset, BA6 9TU
01458 860262

Swaddles Green Organic Farm

Hare Lane, Buckland,
St Mary, Somerset, TA20 3ZB
08454 561768
information@swaddles.co.uk
www.swaddles.co.uk

W N Walford & Co

Upton Bridge Farm, Long sutton, Langport, Somerset, TA10 9NJ
01458 241224
wlafor@globalnet.co.uk

Wallace's

Hill Farm, Hemyock, Devon, EX15 3UZ
01823 680307
sales@welcometowallaces.com
www.welcometowallaces.com

Wild Beef

Hillhead Farm, Chagford, Devon, TQ13 8DY
01647 433433

SCOTLAND

Angus organics

Airlie Estates Office, Cortachy, Kirriemuir, Angus, DD8 4LY
01575 570103
sales@angusorganics.com
www.angusorganics.com

Ardardan Estate

Cardross, Argyll, G82 5HD
01389 849188
enquiries@ardardan.co.uk
www.ardardan.co.uk

Atholl Glens Organic meat
Atholl Estates Office, Blair Atholl, Perthshire, PH18 5TH
01796 481482
info@athollglens.co.uk
www.athollglens.co.uk

Blackface
Crochmore House, Irongray, Dumfries, Dumfries & Galloway, DG2 9SF
01387 730326
ben@blackface.co.uk
www.blackface.co.uk

Connel
By Oban, Argyll, PA37 1PU
01631 710247
sales@saulmore.com
www.saulmore.com

Eastside Lamb
Eastside Farm, Pentland Hills, Penicuik, Midlothian, EH26 9LN
01968 677842
eastsidelamb@aol.com
www.pentland-hills-produce.co.uk

Farmer Sharp
Diamond Buildings, Pennington Lane, Lindal, Ulverston, Cumbria, LA12 0LA
01229 588299
info@farmersharp.co.uk
www.farmersharp.co.uk

Fletchers of Auchtermuchty
Reediehill Deer Farm, Auchtermuchty, Cupar, Fife, KY14 7HS
01337 828369
fletchers.scotland@virgin.net
www.seriouslygoodvenison.co.uk

Mrs Hamilton's Beef and Lamb

Cairns Farm Kirknewton, West Lothian, EH27 8DH
01506 881510
mrshamilton@cairnsfarm.co.uk

Highland Geese

Carranmoor, Ardfern, Argyll, PA31 8QN
01852 500609,
corranmorhouse@aol.com
www.highlandgeese.co.uk

Kirkton Farm Lamb

Kirkton Farm, Milton Bridge, Penicuik, Midlothian, EH26 0PP
01968 674282

Macbeths

11 Tolbooth Street, Forres, Moray, IV36 1PH
01309 672254
info@macbeths.com
www.macbeths.com

The Organic Farm

Newmiln Farm, Tibbermore, Perth, PH1 1QN
01738 730201
orders@the-organic-farm.co.uk
www.the-organic-farm.co.uk

Ormsary Farm

By Lochgilphead Argyll, PA31 8PE
01880 770700
meat@ormsary.co.uk

WALES

Bryn Cocyn Organic Beef and Lamb
Llannefydd, Denbigh, Conwy, LL16 5DH
01745 540207
www.bryncocynorganic.co.uk

Bumpylane Rare Breeds
Shortlands Farm, Broad Haven, Haverfordwest, Pembrokeshire,
SA62 3NE
01437 781234
info@bumpylane.co.uk
www.bumpylane.co.uk

Cambrian Organics
unit 2, Horeb Business Park, Llandysul, Ceredigion, SA44 4JG
01559 363151
info@cambrianorganics.com
www.cambrianorganics.com

Graig Farm Organics
Dolau, Llandrindod Wells, Powys, LD1 5TL
01597 851655,
sales@graigfarm.co.uk
www.graigfarm.co.uk

Edward Hamer Ltd
Plynlimon House, Llanidloes, Powys, SY18 6EF
01686 412209
edward@edwardhamer.co.uk
www.edwardhamer.co.uk

Edwards of Conwy
18 High Street, Conwy, North Wales, LL32 8DE
01492 592443
sales@edwardsofconwy.co.uk
www.edwardsofconwy.co.uk
Welsh salt marsh lamb from family run farms

Eynon's of St Clears

Deganwy Pentre Road, St Clears, Carmarthenshire, SA33 4LR
08007 315816
enquiries@eynons.co.uk
www.eynons.co.uk

Llanthony Valley Organics

Maes-y-Beran, Cwmyoy, Abergavenny, Monmouthshire, NP7 7NL
01873 890701
organics@llanthony-valley.co.uk
www.llanthony-valley.co.uk

May Organic Farms

Panteg, Cellan,Lampeter, Carmarthenshire, SA48 8HN
01570 423080
geoff@themay.co.uk
www.themay.co.uk

Min Y Morfa Farm

Borth Crossroads, Abergele, Conwy, LL22 9SB
01745 590524
www.minymorfa-farm-shop.co.uk

Organic-Aran-Lamb

Ffem CwmOnnen, Llanuchllyn, Bala, Gwynedd,
North Wales, LL23 7UG
01678 540603
sales@aran-lamb.co.uk

References

Chapter 1. Lost riches

1 Cabinet Office Strategy Unit, "Food Matters", July 2008. www.cabinetoffice.gov.uk/strategy/food
2 Office for National Statistics, *Environmental Accounts, Spring 2007.*
3 Richard Manning, *Grassland: The History, Biology, Politics and Promise of the American Prairie,* 1995, Penguin, p. 138.
4 Sir George Stapledon, *The Way of the Land,* Faber and Faber, 1943, p. 181.
5 K. C. Tyson et al., "Comparison of Crop Yields and Soil Conditions During 30 Years Under Annual Tillage or Grazed Pasture", *Journal of Agricultural Science,* Vol. 115, 1990, pp. 29-40.
6 Joe Joseph, "Why Does Science Smell of Manure?", *The Times,* May 29 2008.

Chapter 2. How grass keeps you healthy

1 Weston A. Price, *Nutrition and Physical Degeneration,* Price-Pottenger Nutrition Foundation, 1970, p. 423.
2 Susan Allport, "The Queen of fats: An Author's Quest to Restore Omega-3 to the Western Diet", *Acres USA,* April 2008, pp. 56-62. www.susanallport.com
3 J. Robertson and C. Fanning, *Omega-3 Polyunsaturated Fatty Acids in Organic and Conventional Milk,* University of Aberdeen, 2004.
4 C. Edgar Sheaffer, "Grass Gives Life", *Acres USA,* May 2007, pp. 78-9.
5 D. McDonagh et al., "Milk and Dairy Products for Better Human Health", Teagasc – Irish Agricultural and Food Development Authority. www.teagasc.ie
6 Jo Robinson, *Why Grassfed is Best,* Vashon Island Press, Vashon, Washington, 2000, p. 22.
7 Gonzales Diez et al., "Grain Feeding and the Dissemination of Acid Resistant *Eschericia coli* from Cattle," *Science,* 1998, Vol. 281, pp. 1666-8.
8 www.organicpastures.com
9 Joel Salatin, "The Ultimate Pastured Poultry", *Acres USA,* July 2006, pp. 16-8.

Chapter 3. No more climate change

1 Christine Jones, Australian Soil Carbon Accreditation Scheme, Paper to Katanning Workshop on Measuring the Carbon Cycle, March 2007. www.amazingcarbon.com
2 Rory Carroll and Top Phillips, "King of Soya: Environmental Vandal or Saviour of the World's Poor?", *The Guardian,* March 3 2008.
3 Felipe Fernandez-Armesto, "Stop the Cereal Killers", *The Times,* January 24 2004.
4 Jules Pretty and Andrew Ball, Agricultural Influences on Carbon Emissions and Sequestration: A Review of Evidence and the Emerging Trading Options, Centre for Environment and Society Occasional Paper 2001-03, University of Essex, March 2001.
5 Peterson et al., *The Rodale Institute's Farming Systems Trial: The First Fifteen Years,* Rodale Institute, Penn.
6 www.fcrn.org.uk
7 Methane as a Greenhouse Gas, Media Release from the Rowett Research Institute, Aberdeen. www.rowett.ac.uk/press
8 Tom Phillips, "Milk Production Carbon Foot Print Summary", Pasture to Profit. Phone 07814 483792. www.pasturetoprofit.co.uk
9 Anon., "Glomalin: Hiding Place for a Third of the World's Stored Soil Carbon", *Agricultural Research,* September 2002.
10 www.keyline.com

Chapter 4. How secure is your food supply?

1 David Adam, "Only Intensive Farming Will Feed Britain", *The Guardian*, April 18 2007.
2 "The Salt of the Earth: Hazardous For Food Production", World Food Summit – Five Years Later, Food and Agriculture Organisation of the United Nations, June 2002. www.fao.org/WorldFoodSummit
3 Joel Salatin, "Amazing Grazing", *Acres USA*, May 2007.
4 Robert Elliot, *The Clifton Park System of Farming*, Faber and Faber, 1908, p. 173.
5 William Davies, *The Grass Crop*, Spon, 1952, p. 258.
6 Gene Logsdon, "All Flesh is Grass," in *The Essential Agrarian Reader*, Norman Wirzba (Ed.), Kentucky University Press, 2003, p. 160.

Chapter 5. The deserted countryside

1 James Le Fanu, *The Rise and Fall of Modern Medicine,* Little Brown, 1999, pp.348-9.
2 G. Taubes, The Soft Science of Dietary Fat, *Science,* 2001, Vol. 291, pp. 2535-41.
3 *The Victoria History of Wiltshire,* Vol. 4, Oxford University Press, 1959, p. 28.
4 Sir George Stapledon, *The Way of the Land,* Faber and Faber, 1943, p. 181.
5 George Henderson, *The Farming Ladder,* Faber and Faber, 1944, p. 166.
6 George Monbiot, "These Objects of Contempt Are Now Our Best Chance of Feeding The World", *The Guardian,* June 10 2008.
7 Vandana Shiva, *Yoked to Death: Globalisation and Corporate Control of Agriculture,* New Delhi: Research Foundation for Science, Technology and Ecology, 2001.

Chapter 6. A brief digression on the nature of grasses and grazing

1 R. N. Rudmose Brown, (1912), in Agnes Arber, *The Gramineae: A Study of Cereal, Bamboo and Grass,* J. Cramer: Weinheim, 1934, repr. 1965, p. 332.
2 J. D. Hooker (1854), in Agnes Arber, op. cit., p. 351.
3 D. Griffiths (1912), in Agnes Arber, op. cit., p. 333.
4 H. N. Ridley (1930), in Agnes Arber, op. cit., p. 334.
5 D. B. Johnstone-Wallace and K. Kennedy, "Grazing Management Practices and Their Relationship to the Behaviour and Grazing Habits of Cattle", *Journal of Agricultural Science,* 1944, Vol. 34, pp. 190-97.
6 Andre Voisin, *Grass Productivity,* Crosby Lockwood, 1959, p. 201.
7 Bill Murphy, *Greener Pastures On Your Side of the Fence,* Arriba Publishing, Colchester, Vermont, 1987, pp. 195-6.
8 Joel Salatin, "Amazing Grazing", *Acres USA,* May 2007.
9 Andre Voisin, *Better Grassland Sward,* Crosby Lockwood, 1960, pp. 150-2.
10 Graham Harvey, *The Forgiveness of Nature,* Jonathan Cape, 2001, pp. 149-64.

Chapter 7. Free range milk

1 Jonathan Long, "Effective Control Strategy Keeps Mastitis Bills Down", *Farmers Weekly,* 21 October 2005.
2 A. J. Hosier, Open-Air Dairying, *Journal of the Farmers' Club,* Part 6, November 1927.
3 A. J. Hosier, op. cit.
4 www.organicpastures.com

Chapter 8. Green and pleasant land

1 H. Godwin, *History of the British Flora,* 2nd Ed., Cambridge, 1975.

2 R. G. Jefferson and H. J. Robinson, "Grassland Management for Natural Landscapes and Wildlife", in Alan Hopkins (Ed.), *Grass: Its Production and Utilisation,* 3rd Ed., Blackwell Science, 2000, pp.292-316.

3 R. M. Fuller, "The Changing Extent and Conservation Interest of Lowland Grassland in England and Wales: A Review of Grassland Surveys 1930-1984", *Biological Conservation,* Vol. 40, 1987, pp. 281-300.

4 J. L. Knapp, Journal of a Naturalist, London, 1829; cited in Richard Mabey, *The Frampton Flora,* Century Publishing, 1985, p. 99.

5 Eric Bignal, Davy McCracken and Aeneas MacKay, "The Economics and Ecology of Extensively Reared Highland Cattle in the Scottish LFA: An Example of a Self-Sustaining Livestock System", 2nd LSIRD Conference On Livestock Production in the European LFAs, Bray, Ireland, December 1998.

6 David I. McCracken and Sally Huband, "European Pastoralism: Farming With Nature", European Forum for Nature Conservation and Pastoralism. www.efncp.org

7 "Organic Farms Best For Wildlife", BBC News, 03/08/2005 www.bbc.co.uk

Chapter 9. Designs for a new country

1 www.futurefarms.org.uk

2 www.laverstokepark.co.uk

3 www.lynherdairies.co.uk

4 www.soilassociation.org

5 www.farmfreshmilk.co.uk

Chapter 10. Revolution in the fields

1 Philip Clarke, "Farmers Welcome New US Farm Bill", *Farmers Weekly,* June 6 2008, p. 16.

2 R. Dennis Olson, "Far Bill a Missed Opportunity", Institute of Agricultural Trade Policy Commentary, May 13, 2008. www.iatp.org

3 Geoffrey Lean, "Biotech Giants Demand a High Price For Saving The Planet", *The Independent on Sunday,* June 8 2008.

4 "Patenting The 'Climate Genes' And Capturing The Climate Agenda", Action Group on Erosion, Technology and Concentration (ETC Group), Communique 99, May/June 2008. www.etcgroup.org

5 Mark Moodie, *The Harmonious Wheatsmith,* available from eco-logic books, 19 Maple Grove, Bath BA2 3AF. www.ecologicbooks.com

6 Jerry D. Glover et al., "Future Farming: A Return to Roots?", *Scientific American,* August 2007, Volume 297, No. 2, pp. 66-73.

7 John Vidal, "Change in Farming Can Feed the World – Report", *The Guardian,* April 16 2008.

8 Jared Diamond, *Guns, Germs and Steel,* Chatto and Windus, 1997, pp. 85-92.

9 Vandana Shiva, Globalization and the War Against Farmers and the Land, in *The Essential Agrarian Reader,* Norman Wirzba (Ed.), Kentucky University Press, 2003, pp. 121-39.

10 Jared Diamond, 2005, op. cit., p. 364.

Index

238

242

Stay up to date with the progress of the
grass-fed movement in the UK
by visiting our website:

www.grassrootsfood.com

We would love to hear about any local suppliers
you know and don't find listed in the book.
Hopefully we can include these in a later edition.

Please feel free to share your comments with us at:
grassfed.team@grassrootsfood.co.uk